One Percent BETTER

Make Tiny Improvements for Massive Change Over Time by Becoming One Percent Better Every Day

Leo Black

© Copyright 2020 - All rights reserved.

The content contained within this book may not be reproduced, duplicated or transmitted without direct written permission from the author or the publisher.

Under no circumstances will any blame or legal responsibility be held against the publisher, or author, for any damages, reparation, or monetary loss due to the information contained within this book, either directly or indirectly.

Legal Notice:

This book is copyright protected. It is only for personal use. You cannot amend, distribute, sell, use, quote or paraphrase any part, or the content within this book, without the consent of the author or publisher.

Disclaimer Notice:

Please note the information contained within this document is for educational and entertainment purposes only. All effort has been executed to present accurate, up to date, reliable, complete information. No warranties of any kind are declared or implied. Readers acknowledge that the author is not engaged in the rendering of legal, financial, medical or professional advice. The content within this book has been derived from various sources. Please consult a licensed professional before attempting any techniques outlined in this book.

By reading this document, the reader agrees that under no circumstances is the author responsible for any losses, direct or indirect, that are incurred as a result of the use of the information contained within this document, including, but not limited to, errors, omissions, or inaccuracies.

Table of Contents

INTRODUCTION 1

CHAPTER 1: MEDIOCRITY, GREATNESS, AND ONE PERCENT ... 7

MEDIOCRITY 7
    Mediocrity Influences Those Around You 9
    Choosing Greatness Through Micro-Habits 10
    Working With Anchor Habits 11
    Identifying Key Anchor Habits 12
CHOOSING THE ONE PERCENT HABIT 14
    Applying the One Percent Habit 15
EVALUATE AND ASSESS 17
REALIGN YOUR HABITS 19

CHAPTER 2: PARTING WITH PROCRASTINATION 21

WHAT PROCRASTINATION MEANS FOR GOALS 21
    Decision-Making 23
    Goals 24
NEGATIVE EFFECT ON HEALTH 25
    Exercise 25
    Medical Checkups 26
    Relaxation Techniques 27
    Missed Opportunities 28
    Risk of Reputation 29
    Lack of Self-Esteem 30
    Typical Time Wasters 32
HOW YOU GIVE YOUR POWER AWAY 35
    Baby Steps 36
    Alter Your Workspace 37
    Detailed Timelines and Deadlines 38
    Minimize Habitual Procrastination 39
    Find a Friend 40

- *Decide To "Do It"* 41
- *Choose Motivated Friends* 42
- *Keep Things Simple* 42
- PROCRASTINATION AND PRODUCTIVITY 43
  - *One Thing* 43
  - *Act* 44
  - *Just Five Minutes* 44
  - *Use Music* 45

CHAPTER 3: DITCHING BAD HABITS 47

- TAKING ON TINY HABITS 49
  - *Good and Bad* 50
- IDENTIFYING UNHEALTHY HABITS 52
  - *All or Nothing* 52
  - *All Things in Moderation* 53
  - *Be Kind to Yourself* 54
  - *Be Patient* 55
  - *Changing the Habit* 55
  - *Mindfulness* 56
  - *Remind Yourself* 56
  - *Reward Yourself* 58
  - *Switch Up Your Space* 58
  - *Visualization* 59
  - *Watch Out for Obstacles* 59
- DECIDING TO CHANGE 59
  - *Be Creative* 60
  - *Be Present* 61
  - *Control* 61
  - *Declutter* 61
  - *Enjoy Alone Time* 62
  - *Get Moving* 62
  - *Just Play* 62
  - *Meditate* 63
  - *Pay Attention to Emotions* 63
  - *Spend Time With Nature* 63
- REPLACING UNHEALTHY HABITS 64
  - *Replacing Detrimental Habits* 67
  - *Handling Failure* 67

- REMAINING MOTIVATED TO KEEP GOING 68
  - *Allocate Time* 69
  - *Baby Steps* 70
  - *Don't Set Your Goals and Targets Too Broad or Too High* 70
  - *Be Accountable* 70
  - *Discover Your Purpose* 71
  - *Who's Around You?* 71

CHAPTER 4: RETRAIN YOUR BRAIN 73

- YOU ARE WHAT YOU THINK 73
  - *Get Rid of Negativity* 74
  - *Focus on the Positive* 74
  - *Shift 180* 75
  - *The Golden Rule* 76
- MAKING YOUR MIND UP 77
  - *Change Your Motivation* 78
  - *Being Manipulated* 79
  - *Calendar Countdown* 80
- BREAKING BAD HABITS.. 80
- REPLACE DESTRUCTIVE HABITS 82
  - *Track and Measure* 83
- THE POWER OF POSITIVE MINDSET... 83
  - *Discover Optimism* 84
  - *Become Aware* 84
  - *Develop Resilience* 85
  - *Practice Integrity* 86

CHAPTER 5: TINY HABITS 89

- HABITS CAN CHANGE OUR TRAJECTORY 91
- SMALL HABITS COMPOUND OVER TIME 94
- THE ONE PERCENT HABIT 97
- RESULTS REQUIRE ACTION 99

CHAPTER 6: ACCOUNTABILITY MEANS ACTION 103

- THE IMPORTANCE OF ACCOUNTABILITY... 103
- REPORTING PRODUCES RESULTS.. 107
- ACCOUNTABILITY LEADS TO ACTION... 110

- *Analysis Paralysis*.. *110*
- *Being Bored* *111*
- *Distractions From Others*... *111*
- *Experiencing Stress*... *112*
- *Negative Feedback* *116*
- ACCEPT RESPONSIBILITY FOR BOTH THE GOOD AND THE BAD........... 117

CHAPTER 7: APPLYING ONE PERCENT BETTER..................... 121

- PUTTING IT ALL TOGETHER 122
- CHOOSING GREAT OVER GOOD 126
- THE SECRET TO SUCCESS... 128
- REAPING THE REWARDS 129

CONCLUSION 133

- KEY TAKEAWAY ONE.. 133
- KEY TAKEAWAY TWO 134
- KEY TAKEAWAY THREE 135
- KEY TAKEAWAY FOUR 136
- KEY TAKEAWAY FIVE 136
- KEY TAKEAWAY SIX.. 137
- KEY TAKEAWAY SEVEN 138

REFERENCES 141

Introduction

"Incredible change happens in your life when you decide to take control of what you do have power over instead of craving control over what you don't"

~ Steve Maraboli

Are you REALLY serious about taking control of your conscious life by developing and applying small, micro-changes each day to improve who you are? Don't you wish that you could gain greater control over the circumstances that seem to govern your life, making you happier and more successful? You CAN!!

Do you ever wonder how it is that others seem to know just how to find themselves, while you feel like you keep making the same mistakes over and over again, coming up empty and desperately unhappy with your life, time and time again? Do you feel like you are living someone else's life as though you are just a marionette and someone else happens to be pulling the strings? Read on, and you will learn how to use and apply the same secret weapon of *One Percent BETTER: Make Tiny Improvements for Massive Change Over Time by Becoming One Percent Better Every Day* that top performers are using right now to live happier, healthier, more trouble- and stress-free lives. The secret I am referring to is something that you happen to have had all along—you just do not know how to use it.

What we currently tell ourselves repeatedly in our subconscious eventually becomes conscious and turns into our reality. This includes both our thoughts and our actions. Someone may have planted a tiny seed in your head when you were young that you were exceptionally talented as an artist with an eye for fine detail. You had the capacity to go one of two ways. Either you could embrace this compliment as being true and choose to pursue a life doing what you were always passionate about. Or you could choose to ignore it and battle throughout your life trying to discover what your purpose is. You may have even been bold enough to change careers several times already while trying to discover where you were meant to be.

How you define yourself is purely a result of the habits you have chosen to adapt and adopt into your life. These habits can be both good and bad and will determine the course you are ultimately charting for yourself. What defines a habit in my life is not necessarily what is important to you and, therefore, your habits may be different. Similarities, however, happen when we consider that habits make us who and what we are today.

Let me ask you this:

Are you genuinely happy with your life at the moment, or do you believe that it has the capacity to be better?

Do you have the capacity to be happier or more content than you are now? Are there things that you know you could do differently? Or do you regret certain decisions that you know have turned into bad habits—even destructive ones? Do you believe that you are responsible for the choices and decisions that you have made in your life, bringing you to this exact point in time? Or do you prefer to lay this blame at the door of circumstance, upbringing, education, peer pressure, and so on and so forth (the list is never ending, but exhausting).

I am here to tell you that you are responsible for exactly where you are now! That is true whether you can recognize this for what it is or you are willing to take a few steps back to see what so many others refuse to see. Our habits, good or bad, are what define us and make us who and what we are. So, if we can admit this to ourselves, then why is it so difficult to admit that some of the habits we have right now, that we are tightly clutching onto with both hands, are busy destroying us? Why is it so difficult to let each of these habits go, replacing them with healthier, better ways to live your life each day,leading you to your absolute best life?

Instead, we settle for whatever we have always known because it is comfortable. It is familiar, it is what you have always done, and you are not quite ready to change and see where these new habits take you. Besides, does it not take forever to get rid of bad habits to break down a cycle and replace these with good habits instead? Aren't these massive leaps that need to be taken, rather than smaller, incremental steps? How on earth could you ever get rid of some unhealthy habits that you may have been dragging around with you for a couple of decades?

This is the beauty of *One Percent BETTER: Make Tiny Improvements for Massive Change Over Time by Becoming One Percent Better Every Day.* You do not need to target the entire gamut of bad habits simultaneously, you just need to try for that one percent improvement today over whatever it was that you did yesterday. Sounds a bit simplistic. That is because it really is that simple. You do not need to rush out and get all psyched up because now your life is about to undergo a major overhaul. It is, by the way, but within reasonable time frames. You need to learn how to crawl before you can walk. It is learning to get the baby steps right before you can take on the larger challenges of life.

One Percent BETTER: Make Tiny Improvements for Massive Change Over Time by Becoming One Percent Better Every Day means that you deal with all the small stuff first. You manage to tie down each of these habits and learn to master them before attempting to move on to bigger and better things. It's focusing on the one percent that you can control and change, the one percent improvement that you are able to make, and the one percent adjustment that you can make to getting rid of a less-than-favorable habit. Working slowly and on micro-adjustments daily, you would be amazed at how quickly this can become a compounded effect, influencing different areas of your life.

Another function of *One Percent BETTER: Make Tiny Improvements for Massive Change Over Time by Becoming One Percent Better Every Day* is learning to master habit replacement. It means identifying those habits that are not serving you, that are potentially destructive, time-consuming, and soul-destroying. Somewhere we each have these habits. Perhaps it is that voice in the back of your head that often tells you that smoking is unhealthy for you, but you have been doing it for so many years that you find it difficult to quit. Other habits that can be just as destructive are those of impatience, being short-tempered, or never finding time for your partner or your kids.

One Percent BETTER: Make Tiny Improvements for Massive Change Over Time by Becoming One Percent Better Every Day is going to lay the foundation for you to make small and simple changes to your daily routine and your habits so these are able to compound and become more effective over time. Small and simple changes are manageable, they are doable and will help keep you motivated towards moving forward. The overarching theme of this work is to help you realize that you have within you the potential for greatness. It is being able to recognize where this potential is and then doing something about it.

Within the pages that follow we are going to investigate exactly what sets the one percent apart from the other 99% out there. How can these individuals consistently be more successful, happier, healthier, wealthier, and generally less stressed out than the rest of us? There is no magic bullet or magic pill that you need to swallow.

They see things differently and choose to do things differently. This is what sets them apart and makes them so unique. It is also something that you can embrace as an individual, with minimal effort.

The reason why the effort is minimal is because you are only looking at doing one percent BETTER or one percent more today than you managed to do yesterday. Tomorrow, you will focus on doing just another one percent BETTER than today and so on and so forth. These changes are SUSTAINABLE because you are focusing on small changes. However, as they begin to compound with one another, it begins to get easier to be better. The focus of this work is dealing with micro-changes to make your life that *One Percent BETTER: Make Tiny Improvements for Massive Change Over Time by Becoming One Percent Better Every Day.* With active choice and conscious decision-making, you too can enjoy the benefits of compounded changes in your life. Discover and embrace the small and simple things daily.

Chapter 1:

Mediocrity, Greatness, and One Percent

"Always dream and shoot higher than you know you can. Don't bother just to be better than your contemporaries or predecessors. Try to be better than yourself."

~ William Faulkner

Mediocrity

Why are more and more people in the world settling for mediocrity rather than striving for greatness or an extraordinary life? Why would anyone settle for an ordinary life where they are not sure what they might have done with their life? Because they are neatly nestled in their comfort zone, they are either too scared of failure, or too scared of success. Instead of doing something about it, they choose to hang on to what they know, what is comfortable for them.

These individuals will never truly know or understand what gifts they have to offer the world, society, their families, and most of all themselves. They are happy to keep the mediocrity status quo, rather than rocking the boat and making any change(s) to their lives that just might make it better. Mediocrity means accepting what you currently have because it is as good as it will ever get. It means choosing to settle, rather than pushing the boundaries to the very edge of where they can go. It means being content with your development as an individual as you are now, without trying to see how far you could go if you really gave yourself the chance.

Living a mediocre life means settling for the status quo. It results in personal goals that are easily achievable because that is all that you feel you deserve. You are happy to survive and settle on being average, rather than trying to thrive on greatness. What is holding you back from this achievement is all in your head. When it comes to choosing which path in life you are going to take, you choose the one that has been traveled by many, because the footsteps of others makes it easier for you to follow, rather than opting to choose the road less traveled and leading from the front.

You may even find that setting goals for yourself is a waste of time because you have convinced yourself that you do not deserve anything better than you have right now. It is not about creating a better life for yourself and the members of your family or your loved ones.

Being content has let you see others just like you in the world and you are convinced that this is good enough. You settle for average; you are happy with the mid-level job at the same company where you have been for the last 15 years. Possible promotions come and go, but because somewhere in the back of your mind you have accepted your lot in life, you do not even bother applying for any of these. In your mind, there are better qualified people than you who can do the job better than you.

Your average life seems to be quite normal to you and anything that is going to threaten to disrupt this peace and calm could potentially be harmful (or so your internal dialogue keeps telling you). You may even believe that you need to make some changes to your life, but nothing too drastic because you would rather keep others happy.

Mediocrity Influences Those Around You

Mediocrity is not just a gift that decides to bestow its lack of forward focus on you and you alone, it saps the energy out of anything and everyone around you too. It is choosing to take the easy way out of situations rather than trying to find your passion in life. Mediocrity acts as a thief in the night and can rob you and those around you of the very joy and happiness that life has to offer. It steals precious time with which we must make the absolute best of ourselves, forcing us to settle for less than we are capable of.

Settling for a life of mediocrity is accepting that your life will be nothing more than it is now. It is being happy with a life that is boring and has no flavor. This level of boredom spills over to those you associate with, making them likely to follow your lackluster mood where nothing seems to create a spark of enthusiasm or joy in your life. It seldom offers a dream of greater things to come, instead, it remains focused on acceptance of your current lot that you need to carry around with you indefinitely. Mediocrity is the chain that binds you to remaining who you are, rather than allowing you to become the person you have always known you could be.

Choosing Greatness Through Micro-Habits

What if I could show you how to break these chains of mediocrity and choose to be great instead? Wouldn't it be worth your while to try and discover the secret of what the one percent rule is? What if I told you that it was only going to take you a few short minutes every single day? Do you believe that greatness can start off so small and snowball into something massive? Well it can and I am here to show you exactly how you too can achieve this by applying this simple strategy to your life daily.

How do you end up being great at anything? Many individuals ask me this question and the answer is simply this: you choose it, you apply it, and repeat. It is having the capacity to be strong enough to decide exactly what it is that you want from your life, breaking these things into manageable goals or micro-habits. Learning to apply each of these micro-habits can be as simple as choosing to anchor them to an existing habit and working on it from there. What do I mean by anchoring them to an existing habit? These are habits that we already practice every day and are not even conscious of anymore. They have become second nature to who we are and are done subconsciously rather than consciously.

Working With Anchor Habits

Some examples of these anchor habits are waking up to your alarm every morning and automatically hitting the snooze button. You know that there is a second alarm that is going to go off, and that is really the one that is going to get you up and moving. Climbing out of bed, you automatically put your feet into your slippers, you make your way to the kitchen and switch on the kettle or coffee machine before letting your pets out. Notice how you do not even need to think about any of these things. These are your anchor habits.

Some other anchor habits may include going for an early morning walk or run before having breakfast, hitting the shower, or getting ready for your day because you have already chosen your outfit the night before. You may watch the news while enjoying breakfast or make each of your children lunch before piling them into the car with just enough time to spare to make it to school on time.

Because this has been an early morning routine for you for a number of years already, you don't even realize that these micro-actions are actually anchor habits that you can use to carry some of your one percent habits in order to achieve whatever it is that you would like to achieve from life. Micro-habits are so small that you hardly even notice them when you begin, and that is why they are sustainable. You are not taking on something that is going to phase out within a week to ten days because you are beginning to feel overwhelmed. Instead, you begin so small that there is really no way that you can end up failing.

Identifying Key Anchor Habits

Now that you know what anchor habits are, I want you to sit down and physically write down which anchor habits you have in the morning, in the afternoon, and in the evening. Try and list at least three to five for each time of the day. An example of an anchor habit in the morning might be taking your dogs for a five- to ten-minute walk around the neighborhood. Another example might be following the same route in traffic while you take your children to school and then driving to the office or returning home.

Afternoon anchor habits may include collecting your children from sporting events and/or other after-school activities and driving them home again. This time may be filled with ensuring that washing is done, dishes are stacked in the dishwasher, and homework assignments are supervised. Notice that while each of these are anchor habits, it hardly appears that you have any time available to add any additional micro-habits at all during these hours.

Evenings see dinner being prepared and enjoyed together as a family, with discussion over important events that occurred throughout the day. You and your spouse may have some quiet time together once all the children are bathed and tucked into bed. You may be in the habit of spending some of this time reading and talking about things that are important to you. Anchor habits could include the reading habit, spending time together, getting your outfit ready for the morning, brushing your teeth or bathing before bed … each of these are things that you're already doing on autopilot without any forethought, planning, or preparation.

Write each of these habits down until you have a detailed list. Remember that some of the things I have identified are specific to me and they may not apply to you at all. Your list should resemble those things that happen exclusively in your life for this plan to work at all.

Choosing the One Percent Habit

The first thing to understand is that the one percent strategy is something that is powerful, yet so few people understand it in its simplest form. One of the best ways to try and describe the one percent rule is to link another action to one of your anchor habits that you have identified for each time of the day. You may have identified five from each time of the day, adding up to 15 different habits each day. I would like you to cut this down to just five in total to begin with. These five anchor habits can be whenever you would like them to be, but try and spread them out so that you are not going to be spreading yourself too thin once you begin compounding your habits.

Take the same notebook that you have written your anchor habits in and mark off the five key anchor habits that you are planning on using. On a separate page, identify some habits that you would like to see either changing in your life (getting rid of potentially bad habits) or others that you would like to develop in your life. Write each of these down in the same notebook—ALL of them. This list could include anything from becoming fit enough to hike in the Rockies this summer, to losing 25 lbs. of your winter fat so that you can fit into your summer wardrobe. You may want to learn something new, like a new language, or work on your physical fitness regime. Whatever it is, be sure to capture everything down on paper. Leave the list overnight and think about what you have written down.

By the following evening you should have some greater clarity and focus about which of the goals that you have written down should take preference. It may be that you are feeling more drawn towards certain goals than others right now and that is also fine. The secret to becoming one percent BETTER is being able to identify exactly what you would like to become better at. Review your list once more and select five of these goals that you are going to tie to the five anchor habits you have already listed.

Once you have accomplished this, I want you to break down each of these goals completely to the point that they are ridiculously small. If they can still be broken down further, then you have not broken them down far enough—keep going.

Applying the One Percent Habit

If one of your goals is to learn a new language, and the anchor habit that you've tied it to is driving the children to and/or from school each day, I want you to find an audio version of the language that you would like to learn and set yourself a micro-goal of learning just one new word a day. Sounds simple enough? That is because as I mentioned before, it really is. This is breaking your goal-setting down to the point where it is so simple that you cannot fail.

For the first two weeks, each day you are going to focus on only one new word a day. You are going to write it down, listen to it repeatedly in the car while you are driving your children to school and even practice it with them. By the end of the two weeks, you will have learned 14 new words in this language. Imagine for a moment that you have chosen to learn how to speak French because you are looking to expand your business into the Canadian market, and you believe that this will be beneficial to you. This is your reason behind setting up the goal in the first instance—or your WHY. When your reason is strong enough, you will find that you are prepared to put in the extra effort to see your goal coming to fruition.

After the two weeks, you can begin adding a second word to each day for another two weeks. Write them down on sticky notes and stick them on your refrigerator, your bathroom mirror, your closet, and even in your car on the steering wheel. By the end of this time you will have added another 14 words to the 14 you already have, making a total of 28 French words. Measure your success and share your success with those closest to you. This is now going to take on a snowball effect. In weeks five and six you are going to add three words instead of the two words. Can you see how this will give you another 42 words and you have already tripled where you were two weeks ago? This is the beauty of compounding and doing what you can manage.

Evaluate and Assess

If at any time you begin to feel that the three words are too much once added to all the other words, then cut back and revert to only two words each week. The whole aim of working the one percent rule is that it is manageable and sustainable, rather than placing you under undue pressure. It should be something that you are genuinely interested about, otherwise you will not follow through with it and/or you will become frustrated by the additional habit being added to your anchor habit. Maybe you are a fast learner and three words in a week are too few. Feel free to then kick it up a notch, but remember that the focus is not on how much you are able to do, but rather the simplicity of the goal instead.

You may wish you could change your eating habits and that of your family and have no idea where to begin. Once again, discover WHY you would like to add this to your one percent goals. Is it because you are worried about the obesity statistics in America and you really want to save your family from diseases that are intricately linked with obesity? Or is it because you have noticed that there is a tendency for the family to focus on all the unhealthy food groups and you would like to bring some balance back into the equation? This one percent change needs to be tied to your shopping anchor habit, as well as your "fast food" anchor habit. When attempting to introduce a radical new habit into the home, it is important that it has been discussed and you have the buy-in of everyone in the home for it to work and be effective. This is not to say that you banish all fast foods into outer darkness for all eternity, but it means agreeing to cut back to a level where the whole family is comfortable.

Start by cutting back on unhealthy snacks for the first two weeks. This might include potato chips, sugary cereals, and any other high-sugar items that you would typically store in your food cupboard. For this one percent goal to be successful, you will need to be able to replace the unhealthy foods with other snacks that are healthy. You cannot expect your family to go flat-out cold turkey; they will be suffering from withdrawal symptoms, which would be more problematic for you in the long run.

Replace the chips with things like popcorn or make a platter of vegetables and a side dip that they can munch on while doing their homework or watching their favorite show on television. Look for healthy alternatives to snacks that you would normally buy. Some of these include dried fruit and nuts, fruit rolls (which have the potential to be high in sugar), and savory crackers rather than something sweet. Beef jerky also serves as a great supplement and comes in various forms that the children will love.

Changing a diet is like changing an entire lifestyle. You may need to cut back on all fizzy colas and drinks that are high in sugar and other preservatives. Look for alternatives or buy each member of the household a fancy water bottle that they can refill and drink from throughout the day. While this is something that is developed slowly, it could be introduced over time by beginning with two glasses of water a day for a week, adding an additional glass each week until you reach the minimum amount of water that each member of the family should consume. You could really get creative with this and set up a water drinking contest, with a graph on the refrigerator or some common area of the home.

Realign Your Habits

By the end of a relatively short period of time, you should be able to confirm whether the micro-habits you have chosen to align with your anchor habits are working for you or not. You may discover that it's better to go through your French words while exercising the dog early in the morning because having the children in the car and facing early morning traffic is too distracting to really focus on what you need to. What is important to remember is that these are your anchor habits, and you need to choose what is going to work best for you.

There are no hard and fast rules when it comes to what you should be doing and when you are doing something. The secret to one percent daily habits is that they are so small that you hardly feel like they are habits at all and they have a compounding effect. This means that although you are only doing a tiny bit each day, over time, all the small bits add up to something substantial. Another key to these habits is that they are sustainable because they are so small. You hardly feel at all like you are working on changing a habit or developing a new one.

The key takeaway from this chapter is that choosing to improve yourself by just one percent each day has the ability to compound over time. Because you are only looking at one percent, this figure is manageable and sustainable. You aren't looking to climb Mount Everest just yet. You are learning to take the baby steps that will eventually bring you to that point, yet that's not currently the goal. At the moment, you are focused on getting that single step in the right direction mastered.

Chapter 2:

Parting With Procrastination

"Know the true value of time; snatch, seize, and enjoy every moment of it. No idleness, no laziness, no procrastination: never put off till tomorrow what you can do today."

~ Philip Stanhope, 4th Earle of Chesterfield

What Procrastination Means for Goals

According to Steve Spring from Medium.com, some 20% of all Americans suffer from chronic procrastination. Admittedly, there are a couple of different forms that procrastination takes. From trying to avoid the task completely to leaving things to the last minute, procrastination can take on a whole new meaning depending on whether you're outside looking in or part of the problem. Procrastination is often considered to be laziness, but the two are completely different. Procrastination is finding something else to keep you busy—anything else, instead of the things that you really should be doing. Some of these actions include watching Netflix, surfing the internet, checking your social media accounts, and anything else that you can think of rather than completing the task at hand.

Confusing procrastination and laziness is far from the truth. Individuals who are lazy are not prepared to do anything, whereas those suffering from procrastination would rather be doing something else that's more exciting or more entertaining. Whether we like to admit to it or not, at some stage of our lives we all give in to this typical time waster. Naturally, the degree of procrastination may differ individually, just as we are distinct and unique from each other. Are you able to recognize the signs of procrastination and catch it in time, or do you simply continue on life's journey without readily admitting this to yourself? What makes it such a different yet distinct characteristic? How can you identify it, and what can you do to alter the direction your life is heading in if you feel yourself being sucked into its grasp?

Certified Life and Productivity Coach, Kirstin O' Donovan explains that there are various reasons why people procrastinate and warns of the damage that this habit can cause over continued use. The effects can damage us in ways we cannot begin to imagine. Some of these effects can influence our level of productivity and our life overall. First of all, we are going to look at some of the habits that O' Donovan discussed and then we are going to recommend a teeny, tiny habit that may be able to help you break the mold when it comes to each of these habits. Sound good? Let's dive right in:

Decision-Making

Decisions are almost always negatively influenced when you procrastinate. Rather than coming from a place of strength, where you've been able to weigh all the options or consider all the pros and cons of a decision, you've procrastinated. This places you into an awkward situation where you are now forced into making a decision. The decision is being forced out of you from a position of pressure, rather than having the time to consider all the options carefully. This often results in poor decision-making and regretting choices and decisions made because they had not been carefully considered.

Possible Solution:

Spend 10 to 15 minutes creating a pros and cons list for just one major decision that you need to make today. Carefully review it and then sleep on it. By the morning you should have some clarity as to the course of action you need to take.

Goals

Your personal and/or career goals will be left unfulfilled. Although you know that you need to be moving forward when it comes to setting and achieving goals in your life, you waste so much time trying to identify which of these goals are right for you that you end up doing nothing. There is a wise proverb that says that "the best time to plant a tree was yesterday, the second-best time is today." When you are battling to set and follow through with goals, you may need to determine whether your goals are the right thing for you at this point in your life.

You may discover that you keep on coming up against obstacles and these are preventing you from not only moving forward, but from doing those things that you know are sure to make your life better in the future. If something is preventing you from moving toward these goals, you may need to dig deep to discover what's holding you back. Chances are it has to do with procrastination and you need to be able to break the vicious cycle that trying to set worthwhile goals usually brings with it.

Possible Solution:

As soon as you've written out your goal(s), spend 10 more minutes considering those things that may present as obstacles to hold you back from pursuing your dreams. Write each of these down alongside your goal. Break each of your goals down into such minute, bite-size pieces that there's simply no way you can fail to work towards your goal daily.

Negative Effect on Health

Believe it or not, the seemingly simple presence of procrastination can have a devastating influence on your mental health. This usually starts with a knot in the pit of your stomach because you've missed a deadline (or you're about to). This is often followed by symptoms of anxiety, which lead to depression. Put into simple terms, procrastination can lead to mental health conditions when left unattended for long enough. The cycle starts with stress, leads to anxiety, and carries on to depression.

This is not the only way that stress can negatively influence your health. If you need to change your lifestyle for health reasons, it's unlikely that you will do so if you constantly allow your health to be manipulated negatively. Consider which of these you have put off in the last few months:

Exercise

Is your health currently in decline because you find it challenging to stick with any form of exercise routine? This includes even the most basic exercises such as walking, eating healthy foods, and living the right lifestyle to support longevity. Despite warnings from doctors and other medical professionals, you prefer the sedentary lifestyle rather than actively doing something to change their predicted outcome. You don't seem to grasp the concept of what it will be like suffering from diabetes, chronic heart conditions, or obesity-related illnesses. Nothing seems to hit home for you that you have only one life to live and all the cards are stacked against you when you choose to procrastinate.

Possible Solution:

Set aside your workout clothes last thing before you get into bed at night time and be sure to put them on the moment you wake up. Even if you manage to exercise for two minutes today, you can commit to repeating this action every day. Soon you will be exercising for 20 minutes without feeling like you are sacrificing anything, all because you changed one tiny habit of setting out your workout clothes.

Medical Checkups

You might be accustomed to skipping regular checkups because you don't receive good news and you're tired of all the lectures. You are tired of looking and feeling the way that you do too, but you haven't yet become so uncomfortable with yourself that it's going to drive you to action. You have no idea how important it is to have at least two medical checkups annually if you are suffering from any underlying health problems. It's imperative not to procrastinate with these regular checks, tests, and any other procedures that may be necessary.

Possible Solution:

If you are really that opposed to doctors and specialists, have someone make the appointment on your behalf. That way it is confirmed and finalized, and you cannot easily wriggle out of it. Consider how your health has a direct impact on other members of your family. It's not just about you. If you have small children, they are going to need you to be around for them. If you know that you procrastinate with health-related matters, hand the responsibility to someone who is reliable. Then set reminders on your phone.

Relaxation Techniques

What changes are you prepared to make to take better care of your health so you will enjoy health, happiness, and vitality? You may have decided that taking up yoga will provide you with the best of both worlds. You have found a small, local yoga class that meets up at a reasonable time and it's near enough to travel to daily or three times a week. The same studio offers massages at a really great price and you feel like you may have hit the jackpot. The only problem is getting motivated enough to attend the first class.

Possible Solution:

Ask a friend to join you for a massage, but stress that you need to be there earlier. Arrange for them to collect you (so you cannot chicken out). Set a goal to participate in at least one yoga class each week, followed by a massage to relieve your current stress. You know that you really want the massage, and the yoga class seems to be an excellent trade-off to make this happen.

Missed Opportunities

Have you ever felt like you should have taken a chance on something and you didn't? The truth is that the expression "where one door closes, another one opens" doesn't always hold true for someone who procrastinates. The truth is that once an opportunity passes us by, we aren't always lucky enough to be given the same opportunity again. Life seldom presents us with the same thing on more than one occasion, and if we are too afraid or demotivated to make the very best of every single opportunity presented to us, we may find life slipping away from us.

Possible Solution:

The solution to this problem is to take note of what is happening around you at any given moment and grab each opportunity presented to you with both hands. You will never know how an opportunity is able to change your life unless you reach out and make an attempt to go after it.

Risk of Reputation

One of the things I was taught by my mother was that there was nothing more precious to you than your good name and your reputation. Once you succeed in destroying either of these two treasures, they prove extremely difficult to repair. This is where trust goes out the window because you develop the reputation of being someone who can never see things through. You are known as a chronic procrastinator and you find your reputation tethering on the brink of disaster. So, how can you fix something that seems to be damaged beyond repair?

Possible Solution:

Do everything in your power to salvage whatever goodwill you have around your name. When it comes to procrastinating, set yourself mini-goals that are so small that they won't even feel like you are doing any work. Some excellent examples of this could be when it comes to studying. Set yourself a tiny goal of reading only two pages from your textbook each day. This should take you around five to 10 minutes per subject per day. Depending on the length of the textbook (let's assume that it's about 200 pages), you should be completely done going through your book within just

100 days. Over a year, you should be able to read through the same textbook three times.

In his book, *Atomic Habits: An Easy & Proven Way to Build Good Habits & Break Bad Ones*, James Clear makes an important observation when it comes to actually doing whatever you set out to do … if for some reason you miss a day, don't stress too much about it, but you must pick it back up on the very next day. Skipping two days will kill any chance of you creating a habit from these tiny goals for yourself. For this reason, it's important to continue to follow through with the same tiny goals over the weekend. The secret to turning these tiny habits into successful goals can only be achieved by being consistent. Consistency for 66 consecutive days, to be exact. This is how long it takes for something to become a habit (Clear, 2018a).

Lack of Self-Esteem

Habitual procrastination can negatively impact your career and your life, knocking your self-esteem to an all-time low. If you become identified in the workplace as someone who is unreliable or the person who never gets their work done on time, it's not going to look good on your resume moving forward. It doesn't matter that part of the reason for you not getting your report in on time is that you wanted it to be 100% perfect before you submitted it. Let me share a secret with you about this attitude right now—there is no such thing as being "perfect." Yes, you can submit a document with all the bells and whistles on it, but there may still be flaws, things that you've forgotten to add, or you've been paying such close attention to each myopic detail, that you've lost your way when it came to the big picture.

Possible Solutions:

Try and identify why you feel the need to submit the "perfect" report or document in the first place? What was wrong with your first couple of attempts? What was the real reason behind the delay of your work? Was it really a craving for everything to be perfect, or were you simply waiting for the "perfect time" to actually put your head down and begin? Just as with each of these scenarios, only you would be able to provide the answers. Only you can account for how your work became so caught up in the finer details that you missed the overall objectives. When this happens, you feel like a complete failure, especially if you have been called out regarding the work by senior management in front of your whole team.

Immediately when you receive an assignment, carefully screen it thoroughly to be sure you understand what is required of you. Make certain you are fully on board before you begin with anything. The moment that lines start to blur or become confusing, ask for clarity and get an explanation until you know for certain that you can and will be able to do all things necessary. Your self-esteem and integrity cannot be called into question as long as the lines of communication remain open and you seek confirmation every step of the way. It may seem a bit labor-intensive, but these tiny habits will escalate into much bigger ones further down the line.

Typical Time Wasters

Stop and think about all the things you choose to do rather than doing what you know you should be doing. These are known as typical time wasters! They can be as simple as hitting that snooze button a couple of extra times in the morning when it goes off, to staring vacantly into space trying to figure out where to go next or what to do next. Each of these indicate that you would rather allow situations and circumstances to determine the course that your life takes, rather than you choosing to be actively in charge of what is happening in your life.

Allowing each of these time wasters into our lives robs us of precious time where we could be doing something constructive or worthwhile with our lives instead. Let us simplify each day down to the number of seconds we are each given—86,400! That is it. You can either "snooze" through these seconds by hitting that alarm a couple of times, or you can choose to make them productive.

Imagine that you have an hourglass that has 86,400 grains of sand that only allow a single grain to pass through the narrow neck between the top and the bottom section each second of each day. By allowing that second to slip through, the time is wasted. You cannot magically turn back time and regain those precious seconds (no matter how often we wish we can). The only way to deal with these seconds in each day is to choose to use them wisely. Notice that I have used the word 'choose.' That is because we each have been given agency and choice as to what we do with our time.

What we do not know, though, is exactly how many of these 86,400-second days we have at our disposal. None of us has a crystal ball that can determine when our time is officially up. If this is causing you to rethink your purpose here—some of your actions and choices—then I have succeeded in the message that I am trying to get across in this section! The only thing that we have control over are the choices we make and what we choose to do with the time that we have available to us.

Possible Solution:

From today, from this very second, decide to choose to use the time that you have been given more wisely. That is not to say that you suddenly do not sleep or work throughout the night trying to play "catch-up" to some of the things you may have been missing out on. It is choosing to make better choices with your time. Ask yourself—is there something that I could be doing right now that is more productive than what I am doing? If the answer to this question is 'yes,' then make the necessary changes to your life to become more productive.

One of my favorite books of all time is Mel Robbins's *The 5 Second Rule*. The reason why this made such an impression on me was that her discovery was simple, yet not simplistic. It was something that changed her life (and the lives of thousands of others) almost immediately. Her 'rule' is simply this—when you need to decide on an action of any kind, simply count down, five, four, three, two, one, and make a move! This is probably at the heart of forming tiny habits daily that will eventually have a huge impact on your life (Robbins, 2017).

Whenever you feel your mind wandering, searching for a daydream, pull it back again gently by reminding it how many precious seconds you are potentially wasting by doing so. Practice the 5-second rule if you think that it has the potential to work for you. Whatever you do, try not to waste any more time doing absolutely nothing with your life. You will come to regret these wasted days more than you could ever begin to imagine.

> <u>As a side note:</u> When using the 5-second rule, the countdown needs to begin from five down to one rather than the other way around. The reason for this is purely psychological. If you begin at one and reach five, you can simply continue counting to infinity. If, on the other hand, you happen to begin at five, by the time you reach zero, you need to take some form of action. There is nowhere else for you to go.

How You Give Your Power Away

Chronic procrastinators are always looking for ways to get out of doing those things they know they need to be doing. From finding something that is more "fun to do" to just wasting away the time on frivolous things, it is usually not until the very last moment that you decide to begin the outstanding task. By now you are already beginning to berate and chastise yourself for not having started the work sooner. You are aware that you suffer from procrastination because the feeling that you get in the pit of your stomach every time you choose to follow this course of action leaves you feeling anxious and occasionally maybe even nauseous. One of the worst things for a procrastinator is a deadline hanging over their heads like the sword of Damocles.

We may not want to admit to it, but we each suffer from different forms of procrastination and these happen in varying degrees depending on what else is happening around us. If you are someone who is easily distracted, then find a quiet spot to work, rather than being surrounded by others that you know are going to steal your mojo and keep you from being as productive as possible. Those who are chronic procrastinators live in a loop, according to productivity expert Celestine Chau.

How this cycle works is that they find an excuse to delay putting things off, they do whatever they can to avoid having to do the work until they can no longer ignore it, only to then try and face it. This cycle is then repeated. Each of these tiny habits prevent us from moving forward and is negative. They act as huge obstacles when it comes to achieving any major results in life. Chau shares some of her tips of overcoming these obstacles and increasing your level of productivity at the same time, like:

Baby Steps

Chunk your goals down as far as they can possibly go. Make them so super-tiny that you simply cannot achieve the goal quickly. The ideal time to get the goal done would be within five minutes or less when you initially begin. Remember we discussed how studying just two pages a day could lead you to complete going through your college textbook several times a year by implementing this small and almost insignificant habit.

This goes for any reading that you would like to do daily. It may be meditation, or a means to unwind after a stressful day at the office where you get to enjoy a glass of wine while getting your two pages read for the day. So, what if you are beginning to get into your book and you want to continue reading? Well, there is no hard and fast rule that says that you need to stop after the two pages. Two pages is just the minimum. The other thing is that you should not let your reading become another form of procrastinating from getting other things done instead.

There are other terms for making goals or habits so small that they become super easy to do without even thinking about them and this is known as "chunking down." Essentially what this is, is breaking a major goal, habit, or task into smaller bits that are completely doable. You should not be able to break them down any further once you have chunked them down sufficiently. When our goals are larger than life, they overwhelm us and all we begin to see are obstacles and stumbling blocks.

We identify all the reasons why we should not, could not, or will not be able to achieve the task set out for us. However, once you begin breaking each goal down further and further, it becomes so simple that now you are asking what's going to take so long and what's holding you back from doing it right now. This is the golden moment that you need to get to when it comes to breaking each goal and habit down into baby steps.

Something that is important when breaking your goals down into manageable steps is that you need to complete the first step before moving on to the second and so on and so forth.

Alter Your Workspace

Becoming fully productive depends as much on what is happening around us as what is happening within us. Take a good look around you. What does your desk or workspace look like? Are you surrounded by books, paper, and clutter? Is it an area that is likely to motivate you to work, or send you into a state of lethargy? The reality is that an environment that may have inspired you before can often lose its motivational effect. For this reason, it is important to regularly review and revise your workspace. Give it the odd facelift from time to time, making it as comfortable as possible while still having the capacity to encourage your absolute best effort.

This can be done in small steps. Rather than going out and spending a fortune on an updated workspace, stop and look around your home for things that might encourage you to want to work. Add these items to the wall, your desk, or even to your office chair. Make microscopic changes that will improve your general quality of work and encourage you to continue daily.

Detailed Timelines and Deadlines

When you are going to break your goals down into such minute, tiny pieces, it makes perfect sense that your timelines and deadlines include each of these steps. Rather than working towards one massive goal, you can break your timelines and deadlines down to accommodate these tiny habits. What begins to happen once you choose to go this route is that the big picture is detailed completely on the actual timeline (even though there are much smaller steps along the way). And then you simply have to meet your daily targets for the goal to be successfully achieved. Everything rests on your ability to reach and surpass some of the smaller steps and goals.

Times need to be definitive for these plans to work effectively and for each of the following steps to be achieved. If even one deadline is missed, the entire system will collapse. This is one of the few ways that you will meet those goals that you set for yourself. Anything less than this is simply not good enough and will delay meeting your other targets and objectives.

Minimize Habitual Procrastination

I think we can all identify with habitual procrastination challenges. These are things that we do daily that rob us of those precious seconds that we can never get back again. Examples of some of these are notifications on our social media accounts, or for others of us, emails. The solution to these bad habits can be found by blocking out time that is completely free of any interference. Whether you need to actually turn your phone off during this period or mute your settings on each of your social media accounts, schedule times (such as lunchtime or after working hours) when you can check out what you may have missed out on for the day. I guarantee, if it was anything urgent, people would find a way to get through to you.

What happens whenever we get distracted by notifications from social media, email, WhatsApp, Twitter, Instagram, and so on, is that we automatically stop what we are doing because we suffer from what has become known as "fear of missing out." We have become so addicted to what is happening in the lives of those around us that we neglect to live our own lives to the very best of our abilities.

If you really must leave your phone on, then it may be a good idea to store it in your bag, in a closet, or in another room so you can concentrate on getting those urgent tasks handled.

An interesting fact regarding social media: Did you know that according to a Pew Research study conducted in 2019, more than 74% of all Facebook account holders visit Facebook at least once a day. That is not to say that these all visit Facebook during operating hours, but I know many individuals have it running in the background on their computers all day. This will certainly negatively influence you by preventing you from doing your work.

Find a Friend

I am not talking about winning any popularity contests here. Instead I am referring to finding someone to be accountable to with your goal-setting, planning, follow-through, and providing feedback on a regular basis. This does not need to be someone on your team that happens to be working towards the same thing, it can be anyone who happens to be working towards achieving something. The objective of "finding a friend" is becoming accountable for whatever it is that you are doing towards completing your tiny habits daily, weekly, or monthly. It is finding someone who can motivate you whenever you are not feeling up to doing anything, and you in turn can keep them on their toes. In a sense, this is like having an accountability partner, although they are working on their own aspirations at the same time.

Decide To "Do It"

I bet you didn't know that the famous footwear company, Nike, is actually named after a Greek goddess of victory. Each of her wings were known as a "swoosh," which is what the iconic logo was inspired by when created by young graphic design student Carolyn Davidson in 1971. The total of her invoice for one of the world's most well-known brands today was a mere $35. The first new logo appeared in 1971 on only a single model of soccer cleat, rather than a pair of running shoes as many individuals have assumed. The second half of their iconic logo, the "Just Do It" phrase, has a much darker history attached to it. The creative individual who pitched the tagline slogan to Nike used words similar to those of a serial killer from Utah who, once sentenced to death for his crimes, used the words "let's do it." This soon turned into "Just Do It."

The reason for sharing this story is to show you what can come from small and simple things. Nearly half a century later, Nike is still synonymous with both their trademark swoosh design, irrespective of how simple it is, and their tagline. If someone tells you to "Just do it," I can guarantee that the first thing to spring to mind would be Nike. Maybe you need to have one of their logos handy where you can look at it every day, even if it's your own hand-drawn version on a Post-It note stuck to the front of your computer screen, reminding you to stop procrastinating (Jof, 2020).

Choose Motivated Friends

Choose to surround yourself with people who are like those you would like to become. Chau compares this with being in the company of influential individuals such as Bill Gates or Steve Jobs for just 10 minutes a day. Although this amount of time may seem incredibly short, over time it would compound and result in increased levels of motivation (Chau, 2020). Some of their daily habits and rituals may rub off on you, giving you an advantage over those around you. Be selective in choosing those you associate with both in and out of the workplace. You want them to be a positive influence in your life where they will help you move towards the achievement of your tiny goals and habits. Anyone who is not going to do this is not worth spending your valuable time with.

Keep Things Simple

The entire success of this system of working on improving yourself by just one percent every day pivots on keeping things as simple as possible. By small and simple things great things can be accomplished if that is what you truly desire. Do not overthink where you are and what you are doing once you have broken down each of your goals to the point where they cannot be reduced any further. Try and make every micro-action as simple as possible. Remember that the key is in making things so easy to accomplish that you do not even need to think about them. Your actions should be fluid and almost automatic.

Procrastination and Productivity

We all know that procrastination negatively impacts productivity. It is one of the main reasons why people do not achieve the goals they identify for themselves and end up settling for a life that is nowhere near the life they would love to have. Here are some scientific ways to enhance your productivity immediately by overcoming procrastination:

One Thing

In your myriad of tasks you need to get through in a day, choose just one thing you have been procrastinating on and give that all your attention. Depending on the size of the task, give yourself a realistic deadline to complete this task, making sure that there is no time for backing out or slacking off from getting it done.

Act

The moment you have identified what it is you need to complete, begin acting on it immediately. Do not even think about it. Find somewhere that is comfortable for you to begin and just start.

Just Five Minutes

If you are already overwhelmed by either of the above, break the task down into activities that you can complete in five minutes or less. Once you have done this, pick one of these five-minute tasks and work on it for five minutes. Chances are you will begin to get into the habit of working with these tiny, five-minute goals and before you know it you will be well on your way to completing the task. Whatever you do, do not leave any of these tasks incomplete because your brain will haunt you with it until you do. This is one of the reasons why people suffer from insomnia. They are constantly worrying about everything that they have not done. Another reason to focus on achieving your five-minute goals.

Use Music

Choose an upbeat song that really gets you up and moving. For me, especially when writing, I have a couple of playlists that I really get into the habit of using while I work, either in the background or through my headset. Not only am I more productive when my favorite playlists are on in the background, but I seem to be able to focus on my work a lot better. My productivity is increased with music rather than without. You can decide what works best for you. For some people, music can become yet another distraction, rather than assisting them. Remember that these are recommendations only. Choose to adopt those that are going to work for you.

The key takeaway from this chapter is that procrastination robs you of your ability to get things done as and when they are necessary. Instead of settling back and waiting for the last minute to do something, take control of your life and make things happen immediately. Perfectionism can be one of the reasons for procrastination. While there is nothing wrong with wanting things to be better, being realistic about how much you can do is a key factor in moving forward and making things happen now.

Chapter 3:

Ditching Bad Habits

"Make no mistake about it. Bad habits are called 'bad' for a reason. They kill our productivity and creativity. They slow us down. They hold us back from achieving our goals. And they're detrimental to our health."

~ *John Rampton*

Let's get right down to it. We each have those niggly, horrible habits that we'd rather sweep under the carpet than admit to, right? No matter what we do, we simply can't seem to shake them or get rid of them? For some of us, we are blissfully unaware of these habits until someone politely points them out to us or may even be direct in their approach that we have a problem. Some of these habits may include:

- Addiction to drugs

- Being abrupt or rude with others

- Being addicted to social media

- Collecting junk in the form of clutter

- Compulsive gambling
- Drinking
- Getting into debt
- Lack of patience
- Not exercising
- Overeating
- Playing computer games
- Shopping as a form of retail therapy
- Smoking
- Watching YouTube/Netflix or cable

And the list can go on and on, completely dependent on you as an individual. I'm sure you'll agree that if I were to ask you to identify just five things about yourself that you know are bad habits, you would be able to rattle these off quite easily, without too much thought. At this point, instead of simply asking you to identify five of your bad habits, I would like you to write them down somewhere. Leave enough space between each of these five habits so you can make additional notes. Stick these habits in a prominent place in your home, office, car, bathroom, or wherever you will get to see them at least once a day.

I would like you to begin monitoring each of these habits for two weeks by asking yourself each of the following questions and making notes of the first things that spring to mind:

- What sets this habit off for me?
- Where am I likely to be when these habits strike?
- Is there a particular time of day that's linked to these bad habits?
- Is this habit motivated externally or internally?
- Who else is usually involved when this habit takes over?
- How do I feel when I behave like this?
- Is there something that happens that causes this behavior to occur?

Taking on Tiny Habits

Breaking any long-term habit is going to take time, effort, energy, and a whole lot of tenacity. Rather than trying to do too much at once, look at each of your habits and see how much you can break them down. Having monitored your five bad habits for two weeks, you should now be armed with some vital information for each of them. You can discover anything and everything about the root cause of your behavior by paying specific attention to your bad habits.

This information can be extremely powerful when combined. It could easily show you which of your current habits are most destructive and which should take preference over others when it comes to being broken or replaced. The easiest way to start off small is to break your habit down into each of the bullet points above and see which you can handle first.

Good and Bad

We each possess both good and bad habits. These are formed through basic repetition of performing the same behavior over and over again until it becomes subconscious. An example of this would be brushing your teeth first thing in the morning. Bad habits are often linked to lifestyle choices, although not all bad habits fall into this category. All habits are directly linked to a specific reward. According to mental health professional and clinical psychologist Dr. Timothy J. Legg and author Crystal Raypole, psychologically, all habits begin with three things:

Triggers

These are the things that set off the habit. They usually develop over a given length of time until they become repetitive, creating the habit loop.

Behavior

This is directly associated with the habit you have developed. Especially when these are bad habits. An example of this would be pouring yourself a drink the moment you arrive home from work because you've had a stressful day.

Rewarding the Behavior

This is the reward for completing the habit cycle. Given the example above, while there may not be anything wrong with having a single drink after a stressful day at the office, eventually you begin to see this as the reward. You begin to drink more, which makes you less likeable as a human being. You become irritable and short-tempered with those around you, resulting in your choosing to stop off at a bar on the way home rather than drinking at home.

Can you see how this single drink habit is becoming a habit that can rapidly spiral out of control? The reward where it once relaxed you and allowed you to unwind a bit has now grown into something completely different and is probably starting to impact relationships with your loved ones.

Notice how I have referred to stress as being a contributing factor influencing this behavior? According to Leo Babauta, author of *Zen Habits*, there are only two main causes for bad habits, and these are boredom and stress. When our bad habits become toxic and dysfunctional, the chances are that there are probably other things going on, on a much deeper psychological level, that may need to be explored and dealt with by a professional counselor, psychologist, or psychiatrist (Babauta, n.d.).

Identifying Unhealthy Habits

The definition of an unhealthy habit is anything that can be or has become potentially hazardous to your health or your lifestyle. Anything that's being done in excess has the potential to be added to this list. Here are some of the ways Dr. Legg and Raypole suggest we work through them (Legg & Raypole, 2019).

All or Nothing

Whenever we are looking at changing a habit, we usually look at these actions as being black and white, all or nothing. This is an unrealistic expectation because we know that we are only human. As such, we are subject to many imperfections. Each of these imperfections make us unique and who we are. We may not always succeed in everything we attempt to do, especially when it comes to getting rid of bad habits. What we need most of all, though, is accepting that failure is very much part of the process. Our human side will want to tell us that each time we slip up and make a mistake we should punish ourselves harshly. This would be counterproductive, however.

If you've set in motion a tiny habit of committing to a single pushup challenge each day for 66-days (remember that this is how long it takes to develop a habit), the most important thing to do on day one is complete that single pushup! Everything happens to be going great until you reach day five. It's the weekend and you'd much rather sleep in than get into your gym clothes for your one pushup challenge. All that you need to do today is five pushups and you are done for the day. Is it going to take you less than the golden five minutes? Absolutely. But you can't seem to drag yourself out of bed and so you decide to skip day five completely.

Does this make you a failure at the one pushup challenge? No! You have already completed four days successfully and this has to count for something, right? Rather than berating yourself for failure, or slipping up on one day, consider all the other days that you have been able to make baby steps in the right direction.

All Things in Moderation

Anything taken to the extreme can be hazardous to your health and well-being. Once you begin tracking your habits daily for a while you should begin to see distinct patterns emerge. This will tell you which of your habits are bordering on becoming addictive or could have other long-lasting negative effects on your life. Deciding to change unhealthy habits for healthy ones should also be done in moderation. Anything in excess can be bad for you. You may decide to join a gym or a fitness group by attending a boot camp to lose weight. Anything you become obsessed with has the potential to harm you in the long run.

Be Kind to Yourself

We all know that change can be hard. New habits don't just happen overnight or after successfully implementing them over one day. It takes time, patience, and consistent effort. You can do your best not to slip back into any of your destructive habits, but the truth is that you need to be prepared for this. Your bad habits weren't established over a day either. You may have been smoking or drinking for years already. Suddenly going cold turkey isn't possible for everyone.

Be patient as you try and work your way through the implementation of healthier routines. Don't expect perfection from yourself, this will ultimately do more damage in the long run when it comes to forming positive habits. Failure brings feelings of guilt and remorse. Accept that these feelings will come, but be prepared to deal with them mindfully. You don't need to accept these feelings. You can replace them by trying to identify whether there was something that once again triggered a relapse in negative behavior. Once you know what that is, you're in a better position to deal with it.

Be Patient

Be patient with yourself and give yourself however much time you need to ditch the bad habit to replace it with something better. It's human nature for us to want to wave a magic wand so all our bad habits can disappear in an instant. We would love to replace them with those that are going to be way more beneficial to our health and well-being. Unfortunately, we live in the real world, and habits both good and bad take time to develop. Give it the necessary time that it needs.

Changing the Habit

One of the first questions you need to ask yourself is "Why do you want to change the habit?" Sometimes it's easier to change the behavior when the change you want is valuable or beneficial to you. What are the benefits to you of breaking the habit? Think about this for a while and make notes in a journal. Once you begin listing these things you may begin to see things that you had not considered as beneficial. List each motivation on a piece of paper and stick it somewhere that you can see it daily. The goal is to keep this foremost and fresh in your mind so the changes will become more permanent. This becomes your motivation to keep going.

An example of these habits is cutting back on sweets and drinks that are high in sugar. You can replace this unhealthy habit by replacing sweets with dried fruits and nuts instead and the fizzy drinks with water. All that this is doing is replacing one behavior with another, yet the replacement habit is a much healthier option. It's believed that you can break a smoking habit by drinking an ice-cold glass of water every time you feel the urge to smoke, or include some freshly cut fruits and vegetables such as carrot sticks and sliced apples in your snack box. When that urge hits, grab a carrot stick instead.

Mindfulness

Being mindful can make you aware of your thoughts, feelings, and actions. Mindfulness means simply accepting each habit without reaction or judgment. It's only once you become aware of behaviors associated with the habits themselves that you can search for the triggers that set the wheels into motion that lead to your habitual behavior. It will allow you to think about other ways to deal with triggers, replacing them with better habits. This is an easier way of dealing with habits that can be destructive.

Remind Yourself

Another way to replace harmful habits with good ones is by reminding yourself what your motivation is in the first place. You can do this by leaving messages for yourself around your home. If you have a compulsive eating disorder, you can place some notes on your refrigerator, reminding yourself that you could be doing something else with your time that doesn't involve eating.

There are several things you can do to make minor shifts to your current habits that will make a big difference.

- Do you want to go to sleep earlier, rather than staying awake all night watching your favorite Netflix shows?

- Should you be drinking at least eight glasses of water a day and you find this a challenge?

- Do you keep on losing your car keys?

Whatever the dysfunctional habit is, you can break it by placing reminders around the home for yourself. Keep a bottle of water handy that's always full and remember to take even small sips from it throughout the day. This will increase your water intake levels substantially. Set reminders on your phone for when it's time to turn off the television and retire for the night. Take some time out now to identify some of the habits that you would like to replace with healthier ones and write them down. Remember that they need to be so small that you aren't even going to feel them.

Reward Yourself

A key part of any habit is the reward at the end of the day. Remember that this is the third step in any habit loop. Find an appropriate reward once you have successfully achieved your goal. Celebrate even the smallest of wins. If you manage to get something right that you've been battling with for several days, reward yourself appropriately, even if it's with something small like a cup of coffee at your favorite local café.

Switch Up Your Space

Our habits are often connected to the space that we live in or operate in. How you live, or work can negatively influence your habits. If you work remotely and are surrounded by clutter constantly, you're likely to be distracted. This will cause procrastination with work that needs to be done because your focus will be drawn to the multitude of tasks you notice gathering around you.

Rather than going through the motions and allowing this space to derail you for an indefinite space of time, spend some time tidying up, and create an area that is uncluttered and suitably neat and clean to be able to do your best work in. If you suffer from hoarding or collecting clutter, it may be time to simplify your life and save your sanity at the same time.

Visualization

The power of the subconscious mind and visualization in achieving those goals that are going to be most beneficial to you cannot be overstated. You need to be able to see yourself achieving each of the smaller goals that will lead you towards achieving the main goal. As you begin to visualize things happening, you will begin to feel more motivated to do something about it. Each baby step in the right direction is still progress. When you visualize yourself having achieved your goal, your mind will help you get there.

Watch Out for Obstacles

While trying to swap out bad habits for good, we need to be on the lookout for any barriers and obstacles that might prevent us from moving forward. These obstacles can be anything from our own willpower to pressure from peers and family. However they are dressed up and presented, it's important to be cognizant of them.

Deciding To Change

Half the battle is won once you decide that you're no longer comfortable living life where your bad habits outweigh the good ones. This is where your decision to change comes in. Something to remember when you are looking towards making these changes is that only you can decide when the time to change is right. Your intentions also need to be pure and honorable. Unless you make this decision, you will become bored or disheartened halfway through and give up. As Babauta says, boredom is one of the key ingredients that adds fuel to the fire when it comes to bad habits. Not discovering better coping mechanisms for our stress and boredom can make them almost impossible to break.

There's no single quick cure, habit, or way to break this stress or boredom, but there are ways to reduce it and the unhealthy effects it has on your life. Try some of these on for size? I can guarantee that while you won't find all of them effective, there may be a few that you can begin adopting into your life TODAY!

Be Creative

Way too many of us have forgotten to play as a means of releasing the stress and tension that we carry around with us. Choose whatever creative medium best suits you and get involved in one of these projects rather than choosing to be bored or stressed out. If you know that this usually follows a certain pattern, you could place some of your creative tools within reach.

Be Present

We often choose to live in the past, or a past as we remember it. There's no sense in sacrificing the present and even the future for something that has already happened. These may be positive memories, or they might be completely detrimental and hamper our progress. Take the time to live in the moment. This may take an incredible amount of practice to alter your current mindset, returning it to the present. It is possible, however. Your first choice should always be to live in this moment, right NOW.

Control

Draw up lists of baby steps of things you need to do as a reminder and then begin wherever you feel comfortable. As you manage to complete each task, cross it off of your list and celebrate each small milestone or accomplishment along the way.

Declutter

Take tiny steps when it comes to working with clutter and other important documents. Spending just five minutes daily will compound to making a substantial dent so long as you don't allow the paperwork and clutter to pile up again. Imagine spending your five golden minutes clearing away things that don't belong or throwing out junk that's accumulated over time.

Your five minutes will compound to between 25 and 35 minutes depending on whether you are going to do this every day for a week or simply between Monday and Friday. Focused attention that's intent on completing a task is invaluable.

Enjoy Alone Time

We all dread being alone because this is when our minds take over and we imagine all sorts of things that are not true. Take time out to enjoy this special time with your thoughts. It allows you to process and plan things for your future, for the present, and helps you curb boredom.

Get Moving

Get into a regular exercise routine that will keep you active and motivated. You know your body better than anyone else. Are you someone who prefers working out in a gym, or do you need to be isolated, with just you and the road, iPod plugged in, listening to some of your favorite music? You can tell what exercise routine is right for you and will likely keep you motivated.

Just Play

Many of us take life far too seriously. We have forgotten how carefree it feels to be able to use our imaginations. When we were children there was little that we could not imagine or believe in. Somewhere along the way as we were growing up, we lost this ability to think, dream, and pretend.

Meditate

Set a fixed time each day that is YOUR time where you can think, breathe, and act. Meditation does not always mean that you're focused on a higher power in the Universe, although it could be. You may feel that yoga or Thai Chi are a way for you to get in touch with your inner side.

Pay Attention to Emotions

Remember to be mindful of any stress that you may be feeling and don't allow it to overwhelm you. Focus on your breathing to help you focus on other things that are going to bring you peace and clarity in your life.

Spend Time With Nature

Commit to spending just five minutes each day in nature. Whether this is just walking on the beach, hiking up a mountain, or enjoying the beauty of your own natural surroundings, whatever you choose to do will likely alleviate both stress and boredom.

Each of these examples are different forms of coping mechanisms that you can easily incorporate into your daily routine to help you work your way through the stress and boredom that's leading to your bad habits. Whenever you battle to get to the bottom of what's really causing negative habitual behavior, there may be some deep-rooted anxiety involved. If you can't uncover this on your own, then it's definitely worthwhile speaking with a certified professional psychologist or psychiatrist who specializes in mental health.

Replacing Unhealthy Habits

Author of *Atomic Habits: An Easy & Proven Way to Build Good Habits & Break Bad Ones* James Clear states that "You don't eliminate a bad habit, you replace it." He describes habits that can be physically detrimental to our health such as smoking, drinking, or doing drugs. Other habits may not physically attack us on a biological level, yet they have the potential to influence your productivity. One such habit is monitoring your email the moment you switch your computer on in the morning. This single activity could rob you of hours of your time when you could be most productive (Clear, 2018a).

Getting rid of bad habits is not always as simple as just stopping. It needs to be replaced by something completely different. Instead of checking your emails first thing in the morning when you switch your computer on, draw up an activity schedule where you can allocate some of your lower productivity time to this mind-numbing task. Replace this time with those things that you can be most productive with. This may be attending meetings, making urgent and important calls, writing reports, and so on.

If you know that your productivity takes a dip after lunch, allocate this time to going through your emails. Switch off all notifications on your computer so you won't be distracted by spam and hundreds of other insignificant emails. If you are still receiving emails from a group that you joined five years ago and you don't really even bother with them, it's time for you to unsubscribe and do some tidying up of your inbox.

This is where you can apply either your five golden minutes or another productivity tool known as a power hour. During this time you break your hour into three 20-minute intervals with a five-minute break between for you to take a short break. I have found this to be one of the most effective productivity tools available for getting work done. When you think about it, 20-minute intervals aren't very long to commit to putting your head down and focusing completely on the task at hand. The five-minute breaks are just long enough for you to make a cup of coffee, visit the restroom or take a short walk around to stretch your legs. At the start of the next 20 minutes you are relaxed, revitalized and ready to focus again.

Another technique I use when writing is setting a daily word count goal, breaking that down into manageable chunks, and then setting a minimum time to write daily. Whether this is an hour or five hours, I know what I am capable of and can easily calculate how long it will take to meet my deadlines and timelines. Believe me, this wasn't always so. When I first started writing, I would try and do as much as possible, often falling way short. I would have my editor on my back, demanding my manuscript, which was far from being completed. Something had to give. Then I discovered a couple of worthwhile tips and techniques from other writers out there and the simplicity of what they shared blew my mind.

Do what you can do, as long as you are moving forward each and every day. That was it! No minimum number of words, no pressure. Simply write until you know that creatively you are tapped out for the day. What initially started as a pressurized task that needed to be completed by a certain date turned into a daily passion. I can't tell you how many days I've totally exceeded my goals for the day because the creative juices suddenly began flowing and when you're in the zone you do all that you can to stay there for as long as possible.

In the same breath, on the days when I have nothing left in the tank, I force myself to reach a tiny milestone for the day, such as just 100 words. This keeps me moving forward towards my goals, no matter what is happening around me. I set this as a habit a number of years ago and so far, for seven days a week, I have managed to meet my tiny goal of at least 100 words each day. I no longer suffer from writer's block or procrastination because the goal is so small and manageable that there's no way I cannot achieve it.

Replacing Detrimental Habits

Looking for ways to move past habits that are detrimental to your health often appears as being monumental. Definitely too big to handle on your own. You fail to remember what you were like before you adopted the habit in the first place. You had a life that was free of toxins before you began smoking or drinking. You need to find your way back to where you were before addiction took control of your life. This is not always an easy path, but it definitely is possible.

Handling Failure

You can be your own worst enemy when it comes to failure. It's vital to understand and accept that because we are only human there will be times when we fall and when we fail. The secret to sticking to your tiny habits is moving beyond negative self-talk whenever you fail. The simplest way to move past failures on your journey is by getting up after each time you're knocked to the floor. In most instances, we are our own worst enemies and judge ourselves way too harshly.

Remaining Motivated To Keep Going

Remember that change is both scary and difficult. Many of the habits that you want to change have developed over many years, and some even over a lifetime. Please be realistic when it comes to changing each of these habits. There's no way that the full habit can miraculously be replaced with something else, no matter how hard you may wish for this to happen.

Deal with procrastination and anything else that's preventing you from moving forward. If you find yourself referring to your goals in the distant future, using the word someday, it may be time for you to admit to yourself that someday is actually today. Don't procrastinate for another single day because you are being robbed of the life that you deserve.

Habits guru Leo Babauta explains that we grasp at all sorts of excuses to prevent us from moving forward and towards changing our habits. Some of these excuses include:

- Being afraid of change
- Busyness
- Failure
- Fear of discomfort
- Feeling overwhelmed

- Lack of energy

- Not wanting to fail

- Time

- Uncertainty

- Waiting

We need to realize that each of these are exactly that—excuses! They are the reasons we give ourselves why we're not prepared to give these good habits a go. So, how can you overcome each of these obstacles we've placed in our own way?

Allocate Time

Any change, no matter how small, is going to require time to make the necessary changes. Grab hold of your diary or a calendar and block out certain times of the day or the week where you can work exclusively on your habits. This is more than consistent, daily effort that will compound into something much greater. This is a time where you can track and monitor your progress, sit with your accountability partner and report on your progress, and make tweaks to your routine.

Baby Steps

The whole purpose of working with just one percent BETTER is to work with small, incremental steps daily that will all work together over time. It means keeping each of your changes so small that you avoid feeling pressured into anything. Yet, your actions keep you facing and moving in the direction of your goals whether they are minor goals or part of a much bigger goal. Baby steps help keep you focused on the finishing line.

Don't Set Your Goals and Targets Too Broad or Too High

Goals and habits that are unclear, too broad in nature, or that aim too high will do nothing but create frustration. Any new habits you wish to create should be small enough that you can work on them without too much effort. When you set your sights too high, you can easily become disheartened because you're not seeing the results that you'd ideally like to see.

Be Accountable

Whenever you take on a new habit, be sure that you remain accountable for every action you take to ensure you achieve it. Finding someone who will hold you accountable for each step towards the achievement of your tiny habits will help you to keep each of your habits in the forefront of your memory. It will help you to call each of your habits to your remembrance.

Discover Your Purpose

As you begin this journey of changing your bad habits, swapping them out for positive, healthy, good ones instead, you need to think about your purpose. Why are you doing what you are doing? Do you want to be a better parent? Live a healthier lifestyle? Get out of debt? Whatever your main reason is, this is your true purpose and this should be what will motivate you enough to keep you inching forwards.

Who's Around You?

Those you choose to surround yourself with are just as important. If you truly want to change your entire life, then you may need to take stock of those individuals you are currently associating with. Are they really the type of people you want to be like? Do they have higher standards than you that they choose to live by? A stronger moral compass or code of honor? If not, it may be time to consider severing the ties with each of those friends that are dragging you down. You should only be looking for associations with those you would like to be like.

The key takeaway from this chapter is that habits are formed over time and are a result of both external and internal influences and influencers. We need to understand where habits come from and that bad habits do nothing but hold us back. They can keep us in the past and prevent us from moving forward and becoming the type of person we would really like to become. Do we allow our habits to define us, or are we prepared to go through some pain by changing out our bad habits for ones that will lead to a better, more productive life?

Chapter 4:

Retrain Your Brain

"It takes energy, mental toughness and spiritual reinforcement to successfully deal with life's opportunities, and to reach your objectives."

~ Zig Ziglar

You Are What You Think

Recent studies by Canadian Cognitive Neuroscience expert Dr. Poppenk, published in Nature Communications, indicate that the average individual has approximately 6200 different thoughts daily. Till now, it wasn't possible to determine where one thought ended and another thought began (Cover Media, 2020).

Our positive and negative experiences shape us into who we are now and who we can become in the future. These experiences can drive us towards the type of person we'd like to be, or they can hold us back by incapacitating us completely. Part of this process is a self-preservation mechanism that kicks in. Our natural tendency is to dwell on the negative so that we don't end up repeating the same mistakes over again. Unfortunately, when we allow our brains to rule everything we do, it can prevent us from finding and living the life we deserve.

Get Rid of Negativity

When you find yourself in a negative loop and you're not sure how to get out of it, focus on some deep breathing techniques. Be kind with yourself and admit when negative experiences are holding you back. It's only when you can be fully conscious of your thoughts that you can begin to control them. Breathing in deeply has the ability to change your current mood from one that's negative to a positive one instead. Slow down and focus on replacing each negative thought.

Focus on the Positive

Before you can begin to retrain your thinking, you need to monitor where your thoughts go. Depending on how you process information, some of your innermost thoughts can be stuck in the past, focused on negative experiences. You may need to keep a notebook or journal handy where you can record each of these thoughts. If you are constantly focused on negative events that happened in the past, it may be time to accept there's nothing you can do to change these. It doesn't pay for you to keep revisiting these past experiences. Focus on the present and all the good things you have surrounding you. Whenever you feel your mind wandering to the dark side, find the balance necessary and focus on the positive instead. Look for five small positive things that happen to you each day. Write each of these down and try and identify what led to each positive thing happening.

Shift 180

Whenever you find yourself moving towards negative, self-defeating thoughts, try and shift your focus in a 180-degree direction. As you do this you are going to think completely opposite to where you may currently be. Challenge your thought process by asking, "What is the opposite of this thinking?" If you are feeling guilty, force yourself to feel carefree and innocent. When you feel sadness creeping in, decide to feel joyful and happy instead. If you find it difficult to suddenly alter your feelings, then you may need to practice positive visualization techniques to help you feel this way.

In his bestselling work, *The Seven Habits of Highly Effective People: Powerful Lessons in Personal Change,* author Stephen R. Covey shares an experience he had while conducting research to share with his colleagues at IBM. At the time he had studied hundreds of works spanning more than 200 years, only to discover that the more recent works were all superficial and offered nothing more than a quick fix to individuals. Lasting change however came from what he referred to as "Character Ethic."

Each of these were traits that could be developed over time by forming positive habits such as honesty, integrity, temperance, humility, courage, and justice. He mentions that the autobiography of Benjamin Franklin was a great example of someone who had successfully managed to incorporate these qualities into his life. Years later the "character ethic" began to change and soon became known as the "personality ethic" instead. These habits would occur almost on a subconscious level and become who we are at the very core. They hold our personal value system. And this value system is what we need to be able to reach to make worthwhile, long-lasting changes in our lives (Covey, 1989).

The Golden Rule

We can often shift how we feel about ourselves and others as we practice the golden rule of doing unto others. In today's language we refer to this as being able to pay it forward by showing others small, yet random acts of kindness. This doesn't always need to be directed at those we know. It could be as basic as helping someone across a busy street with their groceries or smiling and greeting someone who looks like they're having a bad day. Each of these things may seem insignificant to you at the time but may make all the difference to the life of the recipient.

Find something that happens to be a strength and learn to share this gift with the world. As you begin to practice this small and simple habit every day, you will begin to notice a change in your own mood as you not only feel lighter and happier, but genuine joy will fill your soul. If you happen to have a particularly good experience practicing this habit, write it down in your journal so you can remember or even reflect on these experiences when you're having a tough day yourself.

Making Your Mind Up

You have the capacity to change how you feel about life, people, situations, the choices you have made, and even your current mood. Part of being able to retrain your brain is choosing to focus and appreciate simple joys happening around you in the moment. Changing your mood can be accomplished by practicing mindfulness. This allows you to focus on the thoughts you're experiencing in the present moment. Where do your thoughts transport you to?

When you are mindful you accept each of these for what they are and simply allow them to occur without attempting to hold them back or judge them as they take place. Being aware of your thoughts brings them into your consciousness rather than your subconsciousness. You can change how you feel by asking yourself what makes you feel happy. Becoming mindful of your thoughts allows you to take control, rather than leaving your mood to chance.

Your aim with mindfulness is learning self-mastery. Before you even allow your mood to become negative identify ways that you can tip the scales in the favor of positive thinking instead. Some of these small, yet effective habits may include:

- Identifying three things that you could feel grateful for and write these down in a gratitude journal

- Is there something you can do that will bring you happiness or joy now?

- Is there something that can bring someone else happiness right now?

As you begin to catch yourself drifting towards a negative thought, stop yourself and attempt to implement one of these techniques instead. It will take some time for this to become a habit, but small steps in the right direction every day will help you keep your thoughts balanced.

Change Your Motivation

It's not a lack of motivation that stops you from moving forward, it's your habits instead. Your motivation strategy is just as important as the goal you want to develop instead. So, what can you do to change your motivation levels? In his book, *The Power of Habit* Charles Duhigg explains that "motivation should be used to build strong, positive habits" (2012). Regardless of how many habits you have, unless you are alert and focused, your motivation may be worthless in assisting you to build bulletproof habits. Habits take anything from 18 to 254 days to develop according to a study published in the Journal of Social Psychology in 2009. Here are some of the ways that we develop habits today:

Being Manipulated

We are all aware that advertising and marketing companies daily do their best to manipulate us subconsciously through subliminal messages in advertising. After a while, though, we actually become immune to their influence because we've seen so many throughout our lives. While you may currently be immune to their effects, the fact is that they do work. This is why advertising agencies continue using them. You can make them work for you by adding small changes to your habit-forming routine. Focus on rewarding yourself. We all like to spoil ourselves with nice things from time to time.

Connect this to a goal or habit that you would like to develop. Associate the achievement of the habit to the reward. This could be something as simple as the one pushup challenge. Once you've been at it successfully for 30 days, follow through with the reward to be sure that you remain motivated to continue. By breaking your goal or habit down into small, manageable achievements your brain should be able to link the two together.

Calendar Countdown

This idea is so simple yet effective that it cannot fail. Take a large calendar that has a block for each day of the month. Find a marker and for each day you manage to achieve your goal, mark the day off of the calendar. The most important thing that you're aiming for using this method is to never skip a day. This can help you push through when things seem to be getting tough and you really don't feel like following through. That big empty space on the calendar will be a reminder to you. Should you slip up over one day, try and continue immediately after. Remember the comment by James Clear, when he describes skipping a second day as the death of a habit. Once you understand this you can program your brain to focus on completing the chain (Clear, 2018a).

Breaking Bad Habits

Remember how all habits consist of a trigger, an action, and a reward? Breaking any bad habits can be accomplished as simply as disrupting and removing one of these three things. Whatever habit you've been stuck with for an indefinite period of time, you have the power to make small but effective changes to break these habits. Firstly, remember to break the habit down to its simplest possible form.

Once you understand what the trigger is and you manage to break this, you will be able to gain control over the habit itself. An example of this would be smoking socially whenever you drink while out with friends. The trigger in this scenario is whenever you find yourself drinking socially along with friends. This leads to smoking as an action, and the reward is feeling good about yourself socially, resulting in an increase in dopamine levels in the brain. You may not feel so great about it the next day.

You're not only dealing with a hangover, but your clothes smell from all the smoke. You feel guilty and anxious because you realize that you've once again fallen prey to one of your bad habits. Dealing with this habit might prove challenging, but if you really want to quit smoking socially you may need to make some drastic decisions and changes to your lifestyle.

Getting rid of the triggers may mean giving up drinking socially with friends altogether or sharing with them that you don't want to smoke at all. Choose one of your closest friends (preferably someone who doesn't smoke) to be your accountability partner in your quest to break this bad habit. While neither smoking nor drinking are suitable to a healthy lifestyle, some people do not have the mental resilience to be able to kick both bad habits simultaneously.

Small, simple actions can make a big difference over time. Each time you choose to refuse a cigarette you are saying yes to a healthier lifestyle. Sure, there will be challenges that will come along with your decision. You may suffer from physical cravings or withdrawal symptoms. As each day passes, however, you will begin to find it easier to say no.

Replace Destructive Habits

Replacing destructive habits successfully lies in our ability to make small inroads and changes. Anything more than this is likely to frustrate us and result in our failure to replace the habit with something better. Start so small that it's impossible to fail. The secret to replacing these habits with something positive is that they need to be sustainable throughout.

Consider for a moment that when you compound a small habit over time you will soon discover that you can accomplish more in a year than if you tried to do a whole lot more and failed after a few days. Keep your efforts small and consistent over time. This is what will allow them to grow much bigger than you could ever imagine. The problem with habits that people try and add to their daily routine is that it's difficult to determine where the finish line is. How much is enough?

Track and Measure

Part of solidifying the tiny habits you are stringing together is to track and measure them daily. Remember that the key to successful habit development is consistency. You can only achieve this when you have accurate records to refer to. Failure is part of your success and so you should be prepared for it. You should also have a contingency plan in place for when you do fail. When it comes to simple habits like spending 10 minutes a day doing yoga or Thai Chi, if you skip a day you need to catch up those 10 minutes. This can be done by either splitting the 10 minutes over two days where you do 15 minutes each, or a single 20-minute slot. The same goes for reading, meditating, or any other positive habit that you are trying to adopt as part of your life.

The Power of Positive Mindset

Creating a positive mindset is one of the ways to embrace positive change in your life. Each of these exercises can be adopted individually, like building blocks that can be added upon in small and simple ways until they compound over time. Remez Sasson describes a positive mindset as, "Positive thinking is a mental and emotional attitude that focuses on the bright side of life and expects positive results" (Sasson, n.d.).

Discover Optimism

Develop the positive mental habit of looking for the good things in life rather than the bad. Life comes with its fair share of ups and downs; we need to accept the reality that we won't always have things go our way. It's developing the habit of looking for that silver lining in every situation. Give yourself time daily to think, plan, and act in ways that demonstrate positive thinking and positive living.

Optimism is developing a form of mental toughness that makes you content with whatever life throws your way and consistently looking for the silver lining in any event. It's choosing your behavior rather than allowing a situation to determine your overall mood. Optimism is learning to be content, rather than wanting more. This is something that is common in society today; nobody is ever satisfied with what they have, and this makes them miserable.

Become Aware

Awareness means being conscious most of the time, rather than sleepwalking through life. It's accepting that people and our relationships are way more important than all the stuff we try and accumulate in our lives. Be aware of your surroundings. Are you surrounded by individuals who are completely negative? This could have a lasting influence on you and your happiness. Choose instead to associate with those who think, act, and feel as you do. Associate with those whose goals in life are positive, and choose not to allow the negativity of others get to you.

Develop Resilience

Resilience doesn't occur overnight. Like most habits, it grows little by little and this is the beauty of focusing on being just one percent BETTER. Being resilient means that you learn to accept things, rather than whining about how unfair life can become. It's picking yourself up each time you fall or fail, without judging yourself too harshly.

Remember that we all have a hard day from time to time and along with every failure comes lessons to be learned. We can either choose to learn these lessons after each time we pick ourselves up and dust ourselves off, or we can choose to wallow in self-loathing and self-pity because we happened to fail.

Some of the greatest successful minds in the world have failed more times than they've succeeded. Part of their success, however, is their ability to bounce back after being knocked down. Resilience is enjoying every opportunity presented to you, no matter what the outcome is. Even in times of failure there is something we can take away and learn from.

Practice Integrity

Integrity is choosing to do the right thing even when nobody's watching. It's being true to your word, your moral standards, and your code of ethics always. Integrity is being honest, with yourself and all those around you. The funny thing about honesty and integrity is that choosing truth and honesty at all times, even in the smallest of circumstances, will give you a peace of mind that cannot be achieved any other way. It's never having to worry about what you have said to anyone ever.

The beauty of integrity and honesty is that the truth will always remain the truth. It's meaning what you say and sticking to it, even when you are forced into difficult circumstances where your loyalty can be called into question. It's choosing to be one percent BETTER today, so that your future will be filled with peace. Integrity is accepting things for what they are, no matter how uncomfortable they may seem at the time.

Complaining about circumstances that are unfair saps your energy and can hold you back from moving forward in the right direction. Integrity is choosing to be true to who you are rather than settling for a life that's more extraordinary to please those around you.

Your brain is not designed to recall fabricated information or lies.

You will always be able to tell when someone is lying to you because certain parts of their story will constantly change. Even the minutest detail should set the alarm bells ringing that information is false. Make tiny daily inroads into practicing integrity. Begin by asking yourself what you would mostly like to be remembered for and work your way back from there.

The key takeaway from this chapter is that both the brain and subconscious mind are extremely powerful and can influence us positively and negatively. We have the power to choose what we think though. What we fill our minds with daily can determine our ultimate destination. Our motivation and mindset may need to be retrained before we can make genuine inroads towards changing our life. It all begins with those thought patterns and processes we focus on most of the time.

Chapter 5:

Tiny Habits

"Our character is basically a composite of our habits, because they are consistent, often unconscious patterns. They constantly, daily, express our character."

~ Stephen Covey

There are distinct psychological reasons for starting with tiny habits rather than tackling major habits head on. If you've ever tried your hand at gardening, especially growing something from a tiny seed or a small seedling, you will know that the process can be quite simple if each of the circumstances are just right.

Your seed needs to be planted in fertile soil that's going to give it all the nutrients it needs to grow. This could be anything from soil composition to the actual spot in your garden where you plan to plant it. You're certainly not about to plant it in a patch that's already filled with debris or weeds. Before attempting to plant anything in this area you would spend some time getting rid of the weeds, uprooting all of the dead plants, turning over the soil to be sure it's aerated sufficiently, and you may even decide to add some supplemental fertilizer.

You will look for the best possible conditions for your tiny seed to have the best chance at survival. Think about what every seed needs for it to grow:

- sunlight

- water

- topsoil

It needs to be nourished and nurtured until the roots can stabilize the tiny seed, allowing it to grow into an established plant. We can compare our large habits to the same process. For them to be sustainable, we need to start off small. So tiny, in fact, that we hardly notice what we're doing at all. The same way we would pull out any dead plants and weeds, we need to uproot our bad habits, clear away any barriers that may prevent us from being successful and give ourselves the best possible opportunity to form tiny habits that can withstand the test of time.

These habits are similar to our tiny seedling. Each starts with a tiny action that forms part of our daily schedule. Only once we have managed to establish our tiny habit can we work towards it becoming a much larger habit that will help us thrive as individuals.

Psychologically when we consider monumental habits, we often feel overwhelmed and end up doing nothing because we are not motivated enough. Experiencing this lack of motivation is nothing new, it's something that we all go through, but it's something we can overcome if we start off small enough. There's power in keeping things as simple as possible.

Habits Can Change Our Trajectory

Part of the reason for keeping our habits as small as possible is so that our motivation to keep working towards the habit or dream remains intact. When we're pushing to achieve something big, we often lose interest in these big habits because it takes forever for us to see genuine movement in the direction of where we want to go. Our habits can change our lives forever, and beginning with tiny habits is the way to do this.

You can change anything from your lifestyle to serving the community, being grateful for what you have and even strengthening the relationships you have with loved ones. Whatever it is that you want to change in your life, you can begin by making tiny changes to habits that you either already have, or you may need to introduce some totally new habits that will bring you that much closer to your overall goal.

If you're currently suffering from couch potato syndrome in the evenings and you know that you should be doing something about it, the simple act of putting on your exercise clothes when you get home could alter the outcome of how you feel towards getting off the couch and away from the front of the television. Set a timer on your watch or smartphone for just five minutes. During this time start walking the dogs, or walk on your own around your neighborhood. Once your alarm goes off, turn around and head back home. Repeat this simple exercise each day for the next month.

Make a note of how you are feeling and whether you are managing to walk further each day. Your five-minute tiny habit has become really simple to do by the end of this period and you may actually be enjoying your afternoon walk, so much so that you may decide to set yourself another goal by adding an additional five minutes to your distance. Your health is beginning to improve, you are feeling healthier and more physically fit. Each time you leave the house you take along with you a full bottle of water, which you sip along the way.

Notice how something that started as a really small habit is beginning to influence other areas of your life. You may have had a problem drinking water during the day because this was always substituted by tea, coffee, or other drinks loaded with sugar. For a long time you've been trying to commit to drinking more water. Thanks to your newly acquired exercise routine, you are now beginning to consume water while you're walking and you're more inclined to pour yourself a tall glass of ice water once you get back home. You're beginning to notice that there are a couple of changes beginning to take place.

You no longer feel so drained when you get back from work. As a matter of fact, you are now beginning to look forward to the fresh air and exercise in the afternoons. You're beginning to pay attention to things during your walks that you normally would take for granted. You enjoy the feel of the sunshine on your face and skin. You now notice the light breeze as it blows from the east. The smell of your neighbor's freshly cut lawn conjures up memories of your childhood and you begin to smile. You notice that there are some roses beginning to bloom along the drive leading to a garage door on your route. There's a distinct smell of flowering frangipani in the air, which holds some pleasant memories for you. You can tell that your mood is lighter, and you feel happier than you have for quite a while.

There's a psychological connection to your mood being lifted and feeling better. There is dopamine being released in the brain, causing you to feel happier within yourself. This means that you are not just getting a physical workout, but it's positively influencing your mental health as well. There's a bit of a domino effect that begins happening from here … you can begin to see relationships improve. Mentally you are able to think more clearly because you are alert and active. Your brain is being stimulated by other things rather than a television.

Small Habits Compound Over Time

If you take the above example where you started with just five minutes a day for a month and then increased it to ten minutes, compounded over 30 days, the five minutes will be the equivalent of two and a half hours working out in a month. Once increased, this figure doubles to five hours in a month. The beauty of keeping habits small is that you don't feel the pressure while you're doing them, but the end result is definitely worthwhile. This is the compounding effect.

Remember how it feels to start a new habit. It's usually the pits, you feel that it's a drag and there's simply no way you're ever going to achieve the end result(s). This is one of the main reasons why dieting fails. We try and change everything about our lifestyle, rather than looking at changing just one small thing for an extended period of time. Once you are happy that the above 10-minute habit has taken root, with the added benefit that you are now drinking at least two glasses of water daily because of your exercise routine, you can try and increase your water intake in other ways as well.

You reach each of these goals by slowly breaking down the major habit. If you are meant to be drinking at least eight glasses of water daily and you've already managed to tie in two, this leaves you with just six glasses to go. One way of incorporating these additional glasses is to have a bottle of water next to your bed during the night. Instead of drinking soda or tea before you retire, sip water from your bottle instead. Be sure to drink a glass of water as soon as you wake up in the morning. This will help replace any of the fluids that your body may have lost throughout the night as it repaired and replenished your body. Do the same with your workspace. Regular, small sips of water can quickly add up to the six more glasses you need to be drinking throughout the day.

Do you understand how compounding works? In financial terms, we all understand that compounding interest on debt is something we try to avoid at all times because it means we get to pay more than we absolutely need to—or that we try to leverage for our investments. Life is all about investing, and therefore compounding interest is a positive thing for your life. Imagine for a moment that one of your goals is that you would like to become better at your job to earn a promotion. How can you go about this without someone leaving the organization? How can you make yourself recognized for what you are doing? How do you become better at your job?

Using a compounding effect there are a whole bunch of things you could do to make yourself better, noticed, and recognized for your efforts. All of these are so simple that you're probably going to kick yourself for not having thought about them sooner. You can start off by adding a few more minutes to the beginning and end of your day. You know how most people arrive at work. They're a bit flustered from the morning rush-hour traffic and it takes them half an hour to an hour to become productive. By choosing to start a few minutes earlier each day, this will not only help you avoid the traffic, but it means you can start your day positively.

Think about your day and plan appropriately to make yourself as productive as possible. A surefire way of being noticed is being productive. This means monitoring yourself for a while to determine where there are peaks and troughs in your day. We all have them. Some individuals are naturally all fired up in the mornings, while others are more productive in the afternoon. Discover where you peak and where you begin to feel low. Plan your productivity accordingly. Plan your day so you complete those important tasks when you are most productive and do those things that could be called busy work when your energy levels are waning. The secret to becoming more productive is knowing yourself.

Use the extra time at the end of the day for two purposes. Firstly, to assess your current day. Did you manage to complete everything you had planned to do throughout the day? How many items are you able to scratch off of your list? Secondly, were there things you never managed to accomplish? If so, make a brand-new list, or keep this handy on your planner or in your diary for the next day. Psychologically it's important to scratch things off a list that you're working from as it gives you a sense of accomplishment and satisfaction.

The One Percent Habit

The one percent habit is simply aiming to be just one percent BETTER today than you were yesterday. Tomorrow, you will aim to be one percent BETTER than you were today. Mathematically speaking, according to Clear, by following this pattern, over a year you will be 37 times better than you are today. That's a significant difference in who you can become. Are you really going to feel that one percent difference, though? Well, the short answer is no, not initially. Choosing to exercise for just five minutes a day is something that's really simple to do and you are definitely not going to even feel it. However, I can guarantee that once you've been doing this for a year, you will notice that there are huge changes that have taken place in your life and it won't be limited to just your physical health. Can you even begin to imagine your physical health being 37 times better than it is now? Doesn't that make you want to put this book down, put your exercise clothes on and start walking, running, swimming, or exercising for five minutes right away (Clear, 2018a)?

Getting back to all the benefits, they may not be immediate, but they are definitely going to be there. Choosing the right thing to do daily will bring huge rewards. Those aches and pains will be gone, you will begin to rebuild muscle where there had been a bit of a spare tire, your energy levels will increase, you will sleep better at night, your ability to concentrate will improve.

There seem to be a whole lot of plus sides to making a small five-minute sacrifice rather than watching television.

One percent better daily is all that's necessary. It's totally doable and sustainable, which is why this is one of the best habit-building methods available. It's focusing on the end result rather than the here and now. It takes instant gratification off the table and replaces it with delayed gratification, further down the line in the future. There are benefits of choosing one percent BETTER daily, most noticeably that the pressure of trying to do it all at once is gone. The changes you are making are incremental and so small that you don't notice them. It's like a flaxen cord that's being woven, one single strand at a time, until it forms an unbreakable bond. The most important part is choosing to do better and be better, rather than accepting the same old outcome that you've always settled for.

Each day we come to various crossroads on life's journey. We can choose to follow the majority down a path that has been battered and scarred by those who have gone before us, or we can choose to forge our own path and work towards our own unique destiny that's meant specifically for us.

Imagine for a moment that you are navigating a sailing ship and your instruments were even fractionally off course. You would need to make some major course corrections to reach your anticipated destination. By adopting the one percent rule, your objective is to chart a better course for yourself, for your life, for your health, for your career, and for every other sphere of influence that you have control over. It's not meant to derail you, instead, it's there to provide you with a life that continues to compound positively over time.

Results Require Action

There is no such thing as wishing and willing things to happen. For us to experience any type of change in the direction our lives are heading we need to put the time and effort in. Taking action that results in the one percent improvement depends entirely on each action we choose to perform. It's completely up to us whether we succeed or fail. We are the masters of our own destiny and as such can determine our own fate. We need to implement a method of reminding ourselves to take the necessary action(s). This could be anything from setting out your exercise clothes before leaving for work, filling your water bottle before you exercise, always ensuring that you have chilled water handy that you can drink from throughout the day. If you're trying to break an unhealthy snacking habit, be sure to add a bag with some nuts and dried fruit to your lunch daily or a healthy yogurt.

Place Post-It notes as reminders on the bathroom mirror, the refrigerator, your office computer, or even set reminders in the form of alarms on your phone. Keep a journal that's up to date or monitor your daily progress on a chart like we mentioned before. If you happen to be walking or running, set your step counter and keep an accurate record of each day's progress. It might be fun to determine how far you've come from the time you start each tiny habit, recognizing that it's compounding over time. The most important thing to do is to realize that nothing is going to change in your life unless you are prepared to make the changes yourself.

The hardest part of this entire process is starting. That's why it's important to make the habit so ridiculously small and insignificant that starting part of the process simply cannot be overlooked. Just like writing this book, progress is made one word at a time, combined into one sentence, compounded into a paragraph and so on. It's breaking down the goal to be able to write just 100 words a day and moving on from there whenever you feel confident and capable to do more. Considering the compounding effect, if this was all that I was doing in a day, I would be able to complete an average length manuscript within a year. This is the beauty of compounding.

While learning to physically act may be challenging for some people, the exact opposite may be true of others. Finding ways to slow down and taking time out to enjoy the sunlight, to breathe in the fragrance of the fresh-cut grass, to stop and hear the birds singing may be a challenge for someone always on the go. Choosing the right actions is what will set you apart from the rest of society. It will be what gives you that one percent edge. There's never been a more important time for you to take control of your life than right at this very moment. The time to choose action is now.

The key takeaway for this chapter is that habits are formed by doing things repeatedly. To change a habit, even slightly, can result in a major shift towards our destination. Even micro-changes to our habits become compounded over time until they become firmly embedded as part of who we are. Once again, our habits are developed by the choices we make. It is no use deciding that you want to change, you need to follow this through with action.

Chapter 6:

Accountability Means Action

"If you are building a culture where honest expectations are communicated and peer accountability is the norm, then the group will address poor performance and attitudes."

~ Henry Cloud

The Importance of Accountability

When I think of accountability, I'm always reminded of the story of George Washington chopping down the family's precious cherry tree. It would have been easy for him to lie and get away with it, he was only six years old after all. He could have blamed a stranger or just avoided the question altogether (although there was plenty of evidence that a little hatchet was to blame). We know that this is just one of the characteristics that made this Founding Father and first American President great.

Accountability means accepting responsibility for your choices and actions regardless of the consequences. It's taking ownership of everything you do. We should be aware that while we have every right to choose and make decisions for ourselves, we don't get to choose what comes along with them. These are what are referred to as consequences, and depending on the course of action we've taken, we could either look forward to a positive outcome or dread the consequences that follow.

You cannot begin to be accountable for anything until you take stock of your situation and analyze where you are currently. Accountability all hinges on ownership. Once you can own your choices, decisions, and actions, you can no longer be a victim to any circumstance you find yourself in as a result of these decisions. It allows you to focus on the results instead. While this is not to say that you will never make a poor decision ever again, it makes you a lot more aware that there are consequences attached to your actions.

When it comes to developing habits, being accountable can help you make positive changes in your life through these five actions:

1. Helping you accept your responsibility in the process

2. It will help you take responsibility for setting deadlines and milestones to reach each habit or smaller goal

3. Ultimately you will be kept on track towards achieving the small habit necessary to accomplish the larger goal

4. You will be able to identify smaller goals to work towards that can become part of the larger habit-forming process

5. You will be prompted each time some action towards achieving each goal is outstanding

In truth when it comes to accountability, there's only one person you could ever hold responsible for the things that happen or don't happen in your life—that's yourself! Accountability gives you control over your choices and your actions. Some of the other benefits of accountability is that it does not hold anyone else responsible for what happens or doesn't happen in your life other than you. Does accountability demand perfection from you in terms of your behavior? The answer to this is an emphatic no. When you choose to act with honesty, integrity, and accountability, you are choosing to take control of your actions entirely.

Productivity can increase as a result of these choices and actions. You can continue to work towards your habits consistently, which is the backbone of being just one percent better today than you were yesterday and one percent better tomorrow than you are today. Rather than restricting you and holding you back, accountability allows you to move forward. It has an empowering influence which helps you achieve success rather than missing the small milestone you have set yourself.

Those who enjoy the greatest degree of success know that they need to be responsible to someone for each of their choices and actions that they take. This is known as an accountability partner and can be anyone within your current circle of influence who is a neutral party. They need to be someone that you like, trust, and can work with, without being too closely connected emotionally. The main reasoning behind this is you need to be prepared to hear negative feedback when this is absolutely necessary. Let's face it, we won't get it right 100% of the time. But that's not what you are aiming for either.

Your goal is that single, small, teeny, tiny one percent improvement today over yesterday's goals or achievements. Together with your accountability partner, coach, partner, or friend you should be able put together a working plan of action, broken into smaller, achievable, and actionable steps. This is the plan that you will use to report your daily, weekly, or monthly progress against. This plan becomes the strategy you will use to get to where you want to be. It will become your blueprint of success.

Reporting Produces Results

Having someone to report back to improves our overall performance. It makes us responsible for our activities, or inactivity. Before you can even begin working with your accountability partner or coach, a strategy of how you plan to achieve each of your goals needs to be designed and developed. The ideal accountability partner or coach needs to be someone you admire and look up to, possibly someone who has already achieved what you're ultimately trying to achieve. The importance of them being completely neutral cannot be overstressed. If you are going to try and work with a friend or close colleague, the chances are that your relationship may not be able to survive some of the more challenging times that you may face as you work towards the achievement of your mini-goals.

There are several things that a great accountability partner or coach will be able to offer you. They can help you measure any progress you make toward your goals. This also accounts for failures or when you just fall short. Remember the warning that skipping two consecutive days of working towards our smaller accomplishments can be the death of the entire goal. This is something that your accountability partner and coach would remind you of.

There's a story of two lumberjacks who were often at odds with one another as to who the better logger was. To put their squabbles to rest once and for all, they agreed to a competition between the two of them to see who could chop down the most trees within a day. Early in the morning, each set out to a different part of a large forest and began setting their axes to the base of each tree, one single blow at a time. Although they weren't in the same immediate vicinity, they could hear each blow as it struck wood, while both men tirelessly worked to prove their strength.

Every hour or so, one of the lumberjacks would become silent for a while before the chopping sound continued. This gave the first lumberjack unprecedented confidence as he continued to chop each tree blow by blow, felling one after another. This continued throughout the day, with the second lumberjack falling quiet for a period. The first began to gloat and revel in the fact that he would definitely be the winner of this particular challenge. By the time they reached the end of the day, to the surprise of the first lumberjack, his opponent had chopped down a great deal more trees than he had.

This puzzled the strong man, and he was hardly able to believe what he was seeing. Eventually, he could no longer hold in his curiosity. Approaching the first, he simply asked "But how? You hardly chopped the same amount of time as I did? This was an impossible achievement for you to beat me." The second lumberjack merely smiled and answered, "Each time I stopped to take a break when you could not hear me, I was busy sharpening my axe."

The moral of this story is simple. If we want to achieve great things, some of the simplest tasks, such as sharpening our metaphorical axes, have the power to allow us to make great inroads simply by making minor adjustments to our methods, or their application. Just as the lumberjack in the story above, we need to learn to sharpen the axe twice as much so that we only need to cut once.

Having someone to report to means that we actually need to be doing something that's proactive. We need to be making decisions, choices, and acting upon them daily. As we do so, we must have someone other than ourselves who is going to hold us to a higher standard every day and demand a progress report from us. Knowing that we need to return with honest feedback to a mentor, coach, or accountability partner daily makes our goals much more realistic. Even reporting on the effort and energy we put into the achievement of our small one percent goals becomes a way to hold ourselves much more accountable.

One of the worst things to happen when it comes to accountability reporting is when it becomes stale. Once we are bored with what was once a shiny new habit, it's difficult to reignite that passion and enthusiasm again. This is why choosing the right individual to provide feedback to is vitally important. Without the enthusiasm to keep us moving towards our small goals daily, there's no point in forming strategies, drawing up charts, breaking down milestones. Your accountability partner needs to be someone who is strong enough to be able to break you out of a slump and a funk more than anyone else. It's preferable that they have previously been to where you are planning on going. They need to understand just how tough the tough times can be.

Accountability Leads to Action

Some of the things that can pull you away from positive, forward-moving action are:

Analysis Paralysis

You may be battling with some of even the smallest of your one percent goals at the moment and this is beginning to lead to a very real phenomenon known as analysis paralysis. For the most part you may have had these feelings under control for many years, yet something small has triggered them. You seem to be slipping back into your old habits and along with the safety net and comfort zone that this provides you with. Having someone tell you to simply snap out of it could have the exact opposite effect. Analysis of where you've gone wrong or failed can be a healthy exercise when managed correctly. This should be done in consultation with your coach or accountability partner.

Being Bored

I think we'll all agree that boredom is an emotion that's not only real, and it's one that probably does the most damage when it comes to achieving our goals. You can be doing everything right and according to plan when habitual boredom kicks in. This is especially applicable when you're working on tiny habits that become routine. You may even feel confident that these habits are so great a part of your life now. You've followed all the rules and you keep track of what's happening (or at least you did). You even keep in touch with your accountability coach on a regular basis. You're still not as fired up as you used to be and even the smallest of obstacles seems to be able to derail you.

A way to break the monotony of boredom is to attach your small habit to something that's interesting or exciting. This will help you combat some of the feelings of being bored. Look for novel or different ways of approaching each habit.

Distractions From Others

Being distracted or tempted away from following through with your goals can set you back in achieving even the most mundane, simple habit. Here are some of the best ways to combat distractions and regain the same level of productivity as before, or even more. Accept that distractions form part of life, but they don't need to rule our lives. Some of the most common distractions include social media alerts and incoming email notifications. For some reason we feel obliged to drop everything else that we are doing to pay attention to the small rectangular device that fits into the palm of our hand or checking your email every time an alert goes off.

Almost 28% of time is wasted thanks to unnecessary interruptions and attempting to return to the original task at hand. For this, you may need to start implementing some small habits to protect you from each of these distractions. One of these could include creating an environment for yourself that is distraction-free. This can be done by closing your office door or separating yourself in your workspace to somewhere quieter. Allocate specific time slots during the day to certain tasks. Turn your phone on silent and place it in your bag or briefcase. Remove it from anywhere that you may be tempted to check your messages, go onto social media, or respond to private messages.

One of my preferred ways of working without distractions is to put headphones on with some of my favorite music on. Not only does the music relax me, but it cuts back on any of the other noise surrounding me in the moment.

Experiencing Stress

There's nothing wrong with experiencing stress from time to time; we all do. How we deal with the stress can be problematic for us. The truth is that there's no such thing as a miracle cure to alleviate stress. What works best for you might not work for anyone else at all. The secret to dealing with stress is different for everyone because we are each unique individuals. Some of the ways to cope with stress because of habits might include:

Keeping a Journal

Journaling has always been a form of release mechanism and one way of being able to offload those things that are worrying us. Especially in times of stress, find some time to journal daily. There are different styles of journaling, from brain dumps to clear your mind of all the stuff that gathers unnecessarily in your brain. Bullet journals are exactly that, brief and to the point words that describe what's happening in your life. Each point could mean something large and important to you, or it might merely be an observation. The final type of journaling is conventional journaling where you use it as a form of a diary. This is free writing, and it can include anything that's currently on your mind. Free writing often has the benefit of helping us vent and offload somewhere safely, rather than specifically directing it at someone. If journaling is your choice of stress relief, set aside the same time every day to sit and write for a specific amount of time. It's important that this become another small habit as this will be a form of a coping mechanism whenever things are looking bleak.

Listen to Music

Slightly more upbeat than journaling, depending on the type of music you enjoy, there's nothing quite like having some upbeat tunes to listen to while you are working, exercising, or even working around the home. If you happen to be feeling stressed out, choose music that you know is going to enhance your mood rather than making you feel more depressed.

Meaningful and Mindful Meditation

Whatever you want to name it, spending time in quiet contemplation can be extremely beneficial to your well-being. This doesn't need to even be an extensive period daily, but you may want to introduce a small 5-minute habit to quiet your mind, revitalize your spirit and improve your overall mental health. What's most important is that you don't need to specifically label it. Most cultures, whether Christian, Muslim, Hindu, Buddhist, or Taoist each practice their own form of meditation already. Find what works best for you and implement a small daily habit to reduce your stress by quieting your mind.

Random Acts of Kindness

Finding some act of kindness that you can perform towards someone else is a great way of diverting your focus from yourself and the concerns that cause you stress. Even strangers may benefit from a kind smile or a warm greeting. Thank those serving you at the supermarket. Send a word of encouragement to a friend going through a hard time. The thing with practicing these small acts is that they don't need to be grandiose, expensive gestures. You don't even need to know the person you're being kind to. The most important part of the entire process is choosing to be kind to someone to show them they are not alone in this world. In the beautiful way that the Universe works, these efforts often come back around, too, and you are likely to find yourself the recipient of someone else's random act of kindness. And the hope that such reciprocal moments produce go a long way toward melting stress since the world begins to look like a more hopeful place to you.

Regular Exercise

Remember to start off really small and manageable. If you suffer from a chronic illness or a disability in any shape or form, it is advisable to get the approval from your general medical practitioner before beginning any strenuous exercise routine. When looking at adding basic short exercises to your routine that won't place strain on your body, keep in mind that they should be beneficial to your health and vitality. Remember to start off with just a 5-minute walk, gradually increasing this effort to 10 minutes. Should you need some low-impact training, you may want to consider swimming instead of walking or running.

Spending Time in Nature

One of the best ways to restore your body, mind, and soul is to spend time in and around nature. This could be anything from going for walks in a forest or hiking up a mountain nearby. It may include finding some natural waterfalls and just quietly listening to the sound of the rushing water as it cascades over rocks. Other ways of spending time in nature might include spending time with your pets or finding the time to walk on a beach if you happen to live near one. Even spending just five minutes daily outdoors in the sunlight can prove to be extremely beneficial to your mental, emotional, and physical health and well-being.

Negative Feedback

Whether we like it or not, there will be times in our life when we receive negative feedback from others. What usually happens in these circumstances is we begin overanalyzing and pulling ourselves apart trying to pinpoint the reason(s) for our shortcomings. When we cannot find them, we begin blaming anything and everything around us, from the weather to the economy, government to individuals. The truth is that negative feedback is what we need to be able to grow. If we are constantly looking to be stroked all the time with positive feedback that creates all those feel-good vibes, then chances are we're not really looking to grow as much as we're looking for approval from others. This has no lasting effect and eventually the glamour soon fades, and we are still left wondering how to get out of the hole to better ourselves.

Not Seeing Results Quick Enough

We live in a world and society that has become so used to everything happening at a fast pace. We feel the need for instant gratification, instant promotion, instant accomplishment in whatever field we have chosen for ourselves. Reality looks somewhat different, however. A need for instant gratification is linked to several of the generations that have grown up in the computer age. They are used to flicking a switch and being able to choose anything their heart desires. Not so much for their ancestors, teachers, trainers, coaches, and mentors, though. They have probably grown up in a very different generation and so they get that anything worth having takes time before it comes to fruition.

It would be like planting our little seedling and expecting it to grow into a mighty oak tree overnight. It's simply not going to happen. Remember that everything takes time to see results, but slow and steady is what will make each result worthwhile.

Accept Responsibility for Both the Good and the Bad

Receiving praise is something we all look forward to because it gives us a sense of achievement, pride, and satisfaction in what we've been able to accomplish. Failure on the other hand is an entirely different story altogether. Before we can move on to accomplishing more small and simple habits, we need to be sure that these two small habits are firmly rooted within us and we have the maturity and enthusiasm to be able to take both the good and the bad.

It involves being able to handle rejection in a constructive way by looking for lessons that you may be able to learn from out of the experience. Professional athletes and other famous individuals spend hours and hours behind the scenes going over the same routine time and time again. Do they stumble and fall? Absolutely! Not that it makes front page news in the tabloids each time this happens, however they often fail more often than they succeed.

All you need to do is go through some biographies of many of the world's most famous and successful entrepreneurs, artists, sportsmen/women, or business gurus. Each will have a golden thread of commonality running through them. They all had to learn by failing a good few times first, before they became successful. Even when many of these individuals seem like they've been born into a life of privilege and therefore they are somehow better than you are, this is simply not true. None of us have control over the cards that life may have dealt us, but we can alter our destiny by making different choices. We can choose to act rather than react. We can choose how we view defeat and failure. Are we going to stay down, pretending that life owes us everything? Or do we get up, dust ourselves off, put a smile on our faces and try once more?

To do this takes an incredible amount of courage, tenacity, resilience, and bravery. Yet it is within each of us to become stronger tomorrow than we are today, simply by choosing to become one percent BETTER.

Some key takeaways from this chapter include that accountability means taking responsibility for your choices, your decisions, and your actions. Unfortunately, few individuals are prepared to take responsibility and accountability for their lives; pointing fingers at others is something that is becoming more and more apparent in society. Yet, assigning yourself an accountability partner means that you are forced to return and report to provide feedback on your progress and even on your failures. Such accountability forces you to act when you feel demotivated or just lack the drive to continue to inch forward. But the person with whom you choose to be accountable should be strong enough to call you out if you deserve it and motivate you to keep trying, especially when things aren't going your way.

Chapter 7:

Applying One Percent BETTER

"When nothing seems to help, I go and look at a stonecutter hammering away at his rock, perhaps a hundred times without so much as a crack showing in it. Yet at the hundred and first blow it will split in two, and I know it was not that last blow that did it—but all that had gone before."

~ James Clear

By now you should be crystal-clear on exactly what one percent BETTER is and how to apply it. In each chapter we have covered various aspects of how you can improve your current situation by identifying and implementing tiny habits. We've also provided you with some of the realities that you may face as you begin applying one percent BETTER as a life strategy. We call it this because it's meant to become part of you as an individual. It should be woven into the very fabric of your being, rather than just touched on lightly. This is the reason why each of your goals should be so small and manageable, so you figure out how to achieve it without having to put too much effort in.

James Clear shares why we each have the potential to succeed with small habits:

> All big things come from small beginnings. The seed of every habit is a single, tiny decision. But as that decision is repeated, a habit sprouts and grows stronger. Roots entrench themselves and branches grow. The task of breaking a bad habit is like uprooting a powerful oak within us. And the task of building a good habit is like cultivating a delicate flower one day at a time (2018a).

We each hold this potential within us. When we choose not to exercise our free will to build a better, happier, and more resilient life for ourselves we cannot hold anyone else accountable other than ourselves.

Putting It All Together

Andrew Ferebee, author and founder of *Knowledge for Men* on Quora, confirmed that there are only two reasons why forming new habits is difficult: first, through lack of understanding how to establish habits, and second attempting to accomplish way too much at the same time (Ferebee, 2018). This is exactly where one percent BETTER comes in. You aren't setting yourself up for failure because your goals are so big that you can't see the finish line.

On the contrary, your goals with one percent BETTER are so small that they seem laughable. They are simple, yet not simplistic. Each one of them is closely linked to something that means a great deal to you. One of the most important things to consider when identifying and implementing these small goals is that they need to be yours. They need to be things that you are genuinely passionate about, otherwise you will soon become bored and lose interest. These two factors have probably killed more goals than anything else. One of the last things you want to be responsible for are goals and habits that are not worthwhile or ones you are not passionate about. You cannot attempt to chase after goals and dreams that belong to others no matter how impressive they may look or sound.

Formulate your own small, micro-habits as well as your plan on how to implement them. This plan should outline each and every baby step necessary for you to see your goal becoming a reality. Give yourself enough time to succeed at cementing your habit. Remember that if you happen to slip up on one particular day you should pick up the pace immediately the following day so lack of interest doesn't set in. It's simple to identify those things that are important to you, but it's not as easy to implement your actual system. This is your actionable items list and how you plan to monitor your progress towards achieving each of your habits.

Apart from the above, one of the next biggest reasons for failing at achieving our goals or setting habits that work is when the broader goal is something totally unrealistic. No matter how well-intentioned each of these goals may be, if they are impractical or humanly impossible to achieve over your desired timeline all that will happen is you'll become frustrated with the entire process. One of the most important keys to becoming one percent BETTER is that it is just one percent. It's not 200% or 400% from where you are now, because those aspirations are completely unattainable.

For habits to work, they need to be approached in a specific way. One that is based on baby steps, rather than trying to participate in an ultra-marathon. Depending on the goal you are trying to achieve, begin in such a way that you know you cannot fail. It's focusing on one percent and leaving the other 99% to fall into place on its own further down the line. Everyone needs to start off somewhere—when it comes to habits, each should be so small that they don't take up much of your time and they are easy to achieve. Here are a couple of small routines that you can try and implement into your life, but only if they happen to resonate with you:

- Create something by using one of your talents.

- Eat together as a family around the dinner table and make this time technology-free.

- Get off the couch and switch off the television. Make some time to spend together with your family, even just for 30 minutes each day. Watch what happens to your relationships.

- Meditate or have some quiet "me-time" for five minutes, either in the morning or evening.

- Read just one page of the novel you bought a year ago and haven't found the time to even begin.

- Spend 10 to 15 minutes journaling each day.

- Spend time in nature, listening to music, take a class, challenge yourself to learn something new each day.

- Take five minutes before bedtime to write three things you are grateful for that happened during the day. This should be kept in a gratitude journal next to your bed.

- Take five minutes to set out your clothes for work before you retire for the night.

- Unplug for a week by taking a social media break. Disconnect your notification settings for all your social media accounts and stick to your decision no matter how tempted you may be to check out what's happening with everyone else out there.

- Your five-minute walk/run/swim routine is only a tiny part of your day.

Choosing Great Over Good

For most individuals in the world, negativity, doubt, and despair surround them and are their constant companions. By working with tiny habits you are able to turn this around, and almost instantly. Here are some of the ways that you can choose to be happy. This, after all, is one of the things that makes for a successful life:

Choose silence. If you have the habit of always complaining at the least little thing, the next time you feel the urge to do so, bite your tongue and choose to be silent. Choosing peace over conflict is not the easiest of things to do, but this small adjustment to a toxic habit can restore peace and harmony into your life.

Choose to use affirmations. Once again, this is another recommendation that some people love working with and others absolutely abhor. If affirmations resonate with you, then choose to set some intentional, positive affirmations that you can switch out over a couple of days. Because you are only focusing on one percent BETTER, don't overload yourself with hundreds of different daily affirmations, choose several that you can put up in different places where you can see them and read them several times daily.

Focus on how your life is blessed. This means doing more than just thinking about it. Physically write it down so when you're not having such a great day you can flip through the pages and begin to recognize all those things you do have.

Keep your cool. Understand that how you approach each aspect and situation within your life is as a result of a choice. You don't need to be one of those individuals who categorically state that they are not morning people. They usually don't manage to snap out of this negative slump until they've managed their third or fourth cup of coffee for the day. Please understand that there's nobody forcing you to be grumpy in the morning. You're choosing to do that all on your own. If you can choose to be negative, you can just as well choose to be exactly the opposite. Remember that this choice is yours. You can wake up earlier and take some time out for yourself to get ready for the day on your own. Use this time to either journal or meditate and see what happens after a while. You'll be amazed at how quickly you're able to shift your mood from negative to positive instead.

Smile. This will tell your entire system psychologically that you are in a state of peace, harmony, and contentment. You have the power to set your own intentions towards happiness. All you have to do is use a couple of muscles on your face and smile more.

The Secret to Success

Author of *The Power of Habit*, Chares Duhigg, is also a specialist in behavioral psychology. He states that the reason people don't succeed with their habits is because they don't reward themselves. Going back to earlier chapters, remember that the third step for any habit is the "reward" that is attached to the action taken. When there's no reward, all that you have is boring, monotonous, repetitive behavior.

There must be a reward attached to the action or behavior that forms part of the habit. Almost all bad habits come with their own immediate reward system because they release dopamine (the feel-good hormone in the brain). Once this is stimulated you feel more and more inclined to continue with this behavior. You can find this linked to most of your bad habits such as smoking, drinking, and being addicted to other harmful chemicals such as prescriptions or over-the-counter medications, which all have this same effect on individuals. Because this reward is instantaneous, the instant gratification monster kicks in, making these habits difficult to break and move away from.

For this reason it's extremely important to set a reward system in place for your small habits, no matter how mundane or simple each of these rewards may be. Some examples of this could include scheduling a manicure at a beauty salon if you manage to avoid biting your nails for two consecutive weeks. Two weeks is doable. It's short enough that the proverbial carrot in front of the donkey is still front and center, but two weeks of not biting your nails for the reward of a manicure might just be what you need to motivate you.

If you've managed to stick with your five-minute walking/running/swimming routine for a month, don't reward yourself with something that's going to pack on some extra weight and make you feel even worse about yourself—find something appropriate that you've been wanting for a really long time and reward yourself with that. Half the fun of developing small, doable habits will be found in the way you choose to reward yourself. Your journaling habit might be well on its way and you may have seen a really neat journal at your favorite bookstore. Set yourself a goal that if you continue to journal each day for the next month you will go in and reward yourself with this journal. Notice how the reward can be closely linked to the goal, although it doesn't need to be. Anything that's likely to keep you motivated and moving in the right direction little by little is worthwhile celebrating.

Reaping the Rewards

The biggest reward that you will be able to see as a result of introducing one percent BETTER into your life daily will be the compounding effect that it has over a year. We're not talking about 37% here. Instead, we're talking about 37 times better! Can you even begin to imagine yourself being 37 times better than what you are today? Maybe that's 37 times fitter, 37 times healthier, or happier. Your relationships might be 37 times stronger than they were a year ago.

Whichever way you slice it, these are some HUGE numbers.

Once your one percent BETTER habits begin taking hold and find roots, you need to be able to take care of them and nurture each one of them until they are strong enough to stand on their own. This is the imagery where I want you to imagine that small seed being planted in fertile soil, being carefully tended daily. Removing any weeds or other obstacles that might prevent it from taking root. This may mean turning the soil over from time to time, watering it, or tying it to a support structure to protect it from being battered from winds and rain. It may also mean covering it with a protective layer when weather conditions are less than ideal.

Tending this small sapling will take time and patience until it's ready to stand on its own, firmly planted in the ground. We are exactly like this seed, or at least each of our habits are like this seed. They need to be nourished and nurtured, carefully protected every single day until what seemed like a tiny habit begins to bloom and grow into something that's compounding daily.

Following each of these processes, we have been able to skyrocket past the average individual on the street. They are still battling to figure out what happened with their New Year's Resolutions from two years ago and why despite having written them down (like everybody recommends), they have still not seen anything happening. The chances are that their goals were so big that they were completely unrealistic.

As we come to the close of this journey, it is our hope that you understand that anything and everything is possible and can be achieved given the right circumstances. Starting off slow and steady is a much better approach than choosing to go flat-out and facing burnout within a short period of time. This leaves the goal in the dust and you feeling completely unmotivated. Chances are, something that may have been achievable will now be shelved indefinitely because you were trying to do too much at once.

It's my deepest desire that you choose to act NOW, not tomorrow, or as part of your New Year's Resolutions for 2021. There really is no time like the present to begin altering the trajectory of your life. May all your tiny habits culminate in the achievement of all of those goals that you've identified as being worthwhile.

The key takeaway for this chapter is, what is "One percent BETTER?" How can you begin to apply each of the themes from the previous chapters together, so they act in harmony and unison with one another? How different will your life be in the future as you begin to apply these lessons to your life? Can you physically visualize changes in your future? Can you identify each of the areas that you know you need to work on? Nobody can answer questions about your personal motivation, where you see yourself, and how you plan to get there other than you. By choosing to be just one percent BETTER today than you were yesterday, you are already ahead of most of the world. If you continue to maintain this momentum daily over an extended period, your one percent will rapidly begin to snowball, spilling over into all areas of your life. You can see BIG rewards by doing small things daily.

Conclusion

"In order to design successful habits and change your behaviors, you should do three things. Stop judging yourself. Take your aspirations and break them down into tiny behaviors. Embrace mistakes as discoveries and use them to move forward."

~ B. J. Fogg

In conclusion, we are going to consider each of the key takeaways from each chapter and discuss how to apply these to your life for maximum results.

Key Takeaway One

Making small improvements each day that equal just one percent can be compounded over time. It's not only manageable because the percentage is so small, but the changes are sustainable over a longer period of time. You learn to take baby steps first, before you attempt to tackle those much larger goals. Your aim needs to be focused completely on getting one percent BETTER each day.

You wouldn't dream of trying to climb K2 without all the right gear and without training for many months, if not years. Before you can learn to run you need to master each of the smaller steps and smaller habits. As you begin to focus on these, you will feel yourself being moved into the right direction.

Key Takeaway Two

We all know that procrastination is the thief of time, but what of the thief of opportunities as well? You need to be the master of your own fate without giving in to this lethargic lifestyle. Whatever your reason for procrastinating, whether it's fear of failure, perfectionism, or possibly even waiting for the right time to start, learn to recognize the signs that you're in a slump.

It's important to get over this mindset as quickly as possible, by realizing that putting things off is not going to get you closer to your small habits. If anything, this will prevent you from moving forward and you're likely to stagnate instead. The time for action when it comes to procrastination is now!

Key Takeaway Three

Anything good takes time to develop. Think about a close-knit relationship that you hold dear. Was it something that happened instantaneously, or did it grow and develop over time? Exactly the same way, any habits worth identifying and developing will be formed over time. These will be subjected to those around you who will either encourage you to push on towards your dreams, or there will be naysayers full of doom and gloom. The habits we develop could be habits of excellence that will propel us towards the achievement of each of our dreams.

Other habits have the potential to hold us back, preventing us from achieving our goals and becoming the kind of person we would really like to become. We should not allow these bad habits to define us and hold us back. Instead, we need to look for ways to live in the present and move forward, rather than being kept in the past. Changing habits can be a painful process, yet a worthwhile one. Are you prepared to make the necessary changes in your life that are going to lead you to a life that's happier and more worthwhile?

Key Takeaway Four

There's power in the conscious and subconscious mind that is able to influence us for either good or bad. Although the mind is so powerful, we can choose what we want to believe and also how we fill it daily. Naturally, if your thoughts are constantly negative and focused on failure, this is what you are going to get. It's understanding that our thoughts control our destination. When we think positively about our habits, we can grow and develop the way we should. We should focus on training our mindset to become more positive. Staying positively motivated is also necessary for us to be able to move forward at any sustainable pace. These habits begin with each of our thought processes. We become what we think and what we focus on most of the time.

Key Takeaway Five

Habits, even mini-habits are formed through repetitive action. That means doing the same thing over and over again that eventually creates a habit. When we decide to change a habit (even ever so slightly) we need to be aware that this can have a major impact on our overall trajectory. Each of these habits compounds over time until they form part of the very essence of who we are as individuals. Choices we make result in the way that habits go. Merely thinking on a habit or deciding that you would like to make your life better by developing some better habits is simply not good enough. Each habit you're trying to develop needs to be followed through with action.

Key Takeaway Six

Taking accountability and responsibility for your own life and where you happen to end up is way more beneficial than doing what most of society does—blaming others. You cannot hold others responsible for the choices, decisions, and actions that you take. Find yourself a reliable, unbiased accountability partner who's not entirely invested in you or your situation. Having a partner means that you are taking your habit-forming responsibility seriously and you're willing to do whatever it takes. You're also willing to work in close collaboration with this individual in creating habits that will produce results.

By taking on an accountability partner you are willing to report on progress made, whether good or bad. They will be able to help you through each of your challenges that you are faced with as you continue to progress with each of your habits. When you choose to be accountable, you understand that your accountability partner sometimes needs to be harsh in order for you to get to where you need to be. Yet you're still prepared to take responsibility for everything that you do or say.

Key Takeaway Seven

In this final chapter there are many questions raised regarding the one percent BETTER habit, putting everything together so each section is able to work in harmony and unison.

- Consider how your life may change in the future as each of these lessons are applied in your daily life.

- Are you able to visualize the changes that take place in your future thanks to implementing the one percent BETTER habit?

- Which areas of your life needs to be focused on first? Remember that you are the only person who can identify each of these areas.

The choice to be one percent BETTER today and each subsequent day that follows gives you a distinct advantage over most of the world. They either don't know that this is able to compound over time, or they're still stuck trying to set goals and habits the wrong way. Continuous momentum over an extended period will see your one percent gaining traction over each area of your life. The end result of choosing to repeat positive habits daily will result in a massive return on your invested time. You will achieve positive outcomes through doing small things daily.

Your time to act is right now, rather than being sucked into the procrastination trap, leaving it for another year or so. This system is so unique and so simple that anyone can do it and make tremendous inroads towards living a happier, healthier life that's miles ahead of everyone else. Don't delay in setting some small and simple habits that will change the trajectory of your life forever. Remember that the only way to change the outcome of your life is by changing some of your habits. Ensure that they're firmly rooted in the ground and begin to nurture each of these tiny seedlings, until they can stand on their own as mighty oaks. The choice when it comes to incorporating these habits into your life lies completely with you.

Here's to living the life of your dreams through small and simple ways!

Leo Black

As a writer it's always important for us to be able to continue to produce our very best work and content that meets your approval. If you've enjoyed this book, please head on over to the review section below and leave a comment.

References

Ackerman, C. E. (2018, July 5). *What is positive mindset: 89 ways to achieve a positive mental attitude.* PositivePsychology.com. https://positivepsychology.com/positive-mindset/

Alton, L. (2019, February 18). *7 Ways to make positive thinking a habit.* SUCCESS. https://www.success.com/7-practical-tips-to-achieve-a-positive-mindset/

Babauta, L. (n.d.-a). *7 Little habits that can change your life, and how to form them.* Zenhabits.net. https://zenhabits.net/7-little-habits-that-can-change-your-life-and-how-to-form-them/

Babauta, L. (n.d.-b). *The habits that crush us.* Zenhabits.net. https://zenhabits.net/crush/

Babauta, L. (2014). *Finding the motivation to change your entire life.* Zenhabits.net. https://zenhabits.net/life-changing/

Babauta, L. (2020). *To create a habit, tell a good story.* Zenhabits.net. https://zenhabits.net/story/

Baller, E. (2016, May 27). *10 Ways to cultivate a positive mindset and change your life.* Tiny Buddha.

https://tinybuddha.com/blog/10-ways-cultivate-positive-mindset-change-life/

Becker, J. (2013, September 3). *12 Intentional actions to choose happiness today*. Becoming Minimalist. https://www.becomingminimalist.com/choose-happy/

Birken, E. G. (2019, May 20). *How habit boredom makes you abandon your goals*. Wise Bread. https://www.wisebread.com/how-habit-boredom-makes-you-abandon-your-goals

Boksic, B. (2013, May 13). *11 Important things to remember when changing habits*. Lifehack. https://www.lifehack.org/articles/productivity/the-secret-changing-habits-successfully.html

BrainyQuote. (n.d.-a). *53 Procrastination quotes - Inspirational quotes at BrainyQuote*. BrainyQuote. https://www.brainyquote.com/topics/procrastination-quotes

BrainyQuote. (n.d.-b). *282 Accountability quotes - Inspirational quotes at BrainyQuote*. BrainyQuote. https://www.brainyquote.com/topics/accountability-quotes

BrainyQuote. (n.d.-c). *Bad habits quotes*. BrainyQuote. Retrieved November 19, 2020, from https://www.brainyquote.com/topics/bad-habits-quotes

Chua, C. (2010, June 3). *11 Practical ways to stop procrastination.* Lifehack; Lifehack. https://www.lifehack.org/articles/featured/11-practical-ways-to-stop-procrastination.html

Clear, J. (2013, May 13). *How to break a bad habit (and replace it with a good one).* James Clear. https://jamesclear.com/how-to-break-a-bad-habit

Clear, J. (2015). *Procrastination: A brief guide on how to stop procrastinating.* James Clear. https://jamesclear.com/procrastination

Clear, J. (2018a). *Atomic habits : tiny changes, remarkable results : an easy & proven way to build good habits & break bad ones.* Avery, An Imprint Of Penguin Random House.

Clear, J. (2018b, November 13). *The 3 R's of habit change: How to start new habits that actually stick.* James Clear. https://jamesclear.com/three-steps-habit-change

Cover Media. (2020, July 20). New study reveals just how many thoughts we have each day. *Newshub.* https://www.newshub.co.nz/home/lifestyle/2020/07/new-study-reveals-just-how-many-thoughts-we-have-each-day.html

Covey, S. R. (1989). *The seven habits of highly effective people : powerful lessons in personal change.* Simon And Schuster.

Fawkes, J. (2017, June 26). *Putting it all together: Your habit change system.* Highbrow. https://gohighbrow.com/putting-it-all-together-your-habit-change-system/

Ferebee, A. (2018, February 13). *The science behind adopting new habits (and making them stick).* Forbes. https://www.forbes.com/sites/quora/2018/02/13/the-science-behind-adopting-new-habits-and-making-them-stick/

Fogg, B. J. (n.d.). *Start tiny | Tiny habits.* Tinyhabits. https://www.tinyhabits.com/start-tiny

Friend, J. (2014, February 3). *The 43 all-time best quotes on change.* Small Steps Big Changes. https://www.smallstepsbigchanges.com/43-alltime-quotes-change/

Goodreads.com. (n.d.-a). *James Clear quotes (author of Atomic Habits).* Www.Goodreads.com. https://www.goodreads.com/author/quotes/7327369.James_Clear

Goodreads.com. (n.d.-b). *Tiny habits quotes by B.J. Fogg.* Www.Goodreads.com. https://www.goodreads.com/work/quotes/67138912-tiny-habits-the-small-changes-that-change-everything

Guise, S. (2013). *Mini habits : smaller habits, bigger results.* The Author.

Haden, J. (2020). *Change any habit painlessly: 6 Tips*. Inc.com; Inc. https://www.inc.com/jeff-haden/change-any-habit-painlessly-6-tips.html

Hardy, D. (2020). *The Compound Effect*. Hachette Go.

Jof, C. (2019, April 23). *9 Surprising facts you didn't know about Nike's swoosh logo*. Designhill. https://www.designhill.com/design-blog/surprising-facts-you-didnt-know-about-nike-swoosh-logo/

Khidekel, M. (2020, February 5). *7 Small rewards that will keep you motivated to stay on track*. Thriveglobal.com. https://thriveglobal.com/stories/new-habit-goals-small-rewards-motivation-tips/

Lally, P., van Jaarsveld, C. H. M., Potts, H. W. W., & Wardle, J. (2009). How are habits formed: Modelling habit formation in the real world. *European Journal of Social Psychology*, *40*(6). https://doi.org/doi.org/10.1002/ejsp.674

Loder, V. (2016, April 26). 10 Scientifically proven tips for beating procrastination. *Forbes*. https://www.forbes.com/sites/vanessaloder/2016/04/15/10-scientifically-proven-tips-for-beating-procrastination/

Mayo Clinic Staff. (2017). *How to stop negative self-talk*. Mayo Clinic. https://www.mayoclinic.org/healthy-lifestyle/stress-management/in-depth/positive-thinking/art-20043950

Meuller, A. (2014, June 13). *25 Tiny habits that could totally change your life*. Lifehack. https://www.lifehack.org/articles/productivity/25-tiny-habits-that-could-totally-change-your-life.html

O´Donovan, K. (2013, June 21). *How to retrain your brain for success*. Lifehack; Lifehack. https://www.lifehack.org/articles/productivity/how-retrain-your-brain-for-success.html

O´Donovan, K. (2014, March 25). *8 Dreadful effects of procrastination that can destroy your life*. Lifehack; Lifehack. https://www.lifehack.org/articles/productivity/8-ways-procrastination-can-destroy-your-life.html

Patel, D. (2017, July 7). *5 Ways to rewire your brain to be positive*. Entrepreneur. https://www.entrepreneur.com/article/296779

Patel, D. (2018, December 12). *7 Proven strategies for overcoming distractions*. Entrepreneur. https://www.entrepreneur.com/article/324560

Perrin, A., & Anderson, M. (2019, April 10). *Share of U.S. adults using social media, including Facebook, is mostly unchanged since 2018*. Pew Research Center. https://www.pewresearch.org/fact-tank/2019/04/10/share-of-u-s-adults-using-social-media-including-facebook-is-mostly-unchanged-since-2018/

Pierce, S. (n.d.). *5 Benefits of accountability to achieve your goals*. Lifecoach2women.com. https://lifecoach2women.com/main/5-benefits-of-accountability-to-achieve-your-goals/

Pinola, M., & Yuko, E. (2019, October 8). *The best ways to break bad habits*. Lifehacker. https://lifehacker.com/top-10-ways-to-break-bad-habits-1694247761

Raypole, C., & Legg, T. J. (2019, October 28). How to break a habit (and make it stick). *Healthline*. https://www.healthline.com/health/how-to-break-a-habit

Salem, C. (2017, September 4). *Why being accountable is important?* Christopher Salem. https://christophersalem.com/why-being-accountable-is-important/

Santi, J. (2020, July 13). *17 Insanely easy habits that will change your life*. The Everygirl. https://theeverygirl.com/insanely-easy-habits-that-will-change-your-life/

Scott, E., & Gans, S. (2019, June 24). *The one thing you can do to manage stress every day*. Verywell Mind. https://www.verywellmind.com/the-most-effective-habits-to-relieve-daily-stress-3144563

Spring, S. (2018, December 16). *How to stop procrastination from ruining your life*. Medium. https://medium.com/live-your-life-on-purpose/how-to-stop-procrastination-from-ruining-your-life-99c26cabdf79

SUCCESS Magazine. (2017, August 17). *17 Motivational quotes to inspire successful habits.* Medium. https://medium.com/@successmagazine/17-motivational-quotes-to-inspire-successful-habits-50da988d90b1

SUCCESS Staff. (2017, July 20). *17 Powerful quotes to strengthen your mind | SUCCESS.* SUCCESS. https://www.success.com/17-powerful-quotes-to-strengthen-your-mind/

Sung, O. (2020, June 24). Habits: The art of compounding choices. *Junto Investments.* https://junto.investments/atomic-habits/

Tract, B. (2016, April 21). *7 Steps to developing a new habit.* Brian Tracy's Self Improvement & Professional Development Blog. https://www.briantracy.com/blog/personal-success/seven-steps-to-developing-a-new-habit/

Wolya, R. (2017, March 7). *The story of two woodcutters —Why you should sharpen your axes.* Screeble. https://screeble.com/blog/2017/03/07/story-of-two-woodcutters/

Young Entrepreneur Council. (2015, April 6). *12 Ways to shift your mindset and embrace change.* Inc.com. https://www.inc.com/young-entrepreneur-council/12-ways-to-shift-your-mindset-and-embrace-change.html

Young, S. H. (2007, August 14). *18 Tricks to make new habits stick*. Lifehack; Lifehack. https://www.lifehack.org/articles/featured/18-tricks-to-make-new-habits-stick.html

www.ingramcontent.com/pod-product-compliance
Lightning Source LLC
Chambersburg PA
CBHW052359220526
45465CB00003BB/1175